THE PSYCHIC BEING

The Psychic Being

Soul: Its Nature, Mission and Evolution

Selections from the Works of
SRI AUROBINDO
and
THE MOTHER

Compiled by
A.S. Dalal

SRI AUROBINDO ASHRAM
PONDICHERRY

First edition: 1989
Reprinted: 1990, 1992, 1994, 1997, 1999, 2003
Second edition: 2008

Rs 70
ISBN 978-81-7058-896-2

© Sri Aurobindo Ashram Trust 1989, 2008
Published by Sri Aurobindo Ashram Publication Department,
Pondicherry - 605 002
Web http://www.sabda.in

Printed at Sri Aurobindo Ashram Press, Pondicherry
PRINTED IN INDIA

But since she knows the toil of mind and life
As a mother feels and shares her children's lives,
She puts forth a small portion of herself,
A being no bigger than the thumb of man
Into a hidden region of the heart
To face the pang and to forget the bliss,
To share the suffering and endure earth's wounds
And labour mid the labour of the stars.
This in us laughs and weeps, suffers the stroke,
Exults in victory, struggles for the crown;
Identified with the mind and body and life,
It takes on itself their anguish and defeat,
Bleeds with Fate's whips and hangs upon the cross,
Yet is the unwounded and immortal self
Supporting the actor in the human scene.
Through this she sends us her glory and her powers,
Pushes to wisdom's heights, through misery's gulfs;
She gives us strength to do our daily task
And sympathy that partakes of others' grief
And the little strength we have to help our race,
We who must fill the role of the universe
Acting itself out in a slight human shape
And on our shoulders carry the struggling world.
This is in us the godhead small and marred;
In this human portion of divinity
She seats the greatness of the Soul in Time
To uplift from light to light, from power to power,
Till on a heavenly peak it stands, a king.
In body weak, in its heart an invincible might,
It climbs stumbling, held up by an unseen hand,
A toiling spirit in a mortal shape.

Sri Aurobindo
Savitri, Book VII, Canto V

CONTENTS

Preface ... i

SECTION I

Meaning and Nature of the Psychic Being

What is Meant by the Psychic Being	... 3
Atman, Jivatman and the Psychic	... 13
Psychic-Mental, Psychic-Vital, Psychic-Physical	... 21
The Double Soul	... 24
Nature of the Psychic Being	... 28
The Psychic and the Spiritual	... 36
Emotion and Love — Vital and Psychic	... 39
Knowledge — Mental and Psychic	... 43

SECTION II

Role, Function and Action of the Psychic

Function of the Psychic	... 49
Influence and Action of the Psychic	... 52
Guidance through Organisation of Life	... 60
The Psychic Being — Centre for Self-Unification	... 67

SECTION III

Growth and Development of the Psychic

Evolution and the Psychic	... 75
Process of Psychic Growth and Development	... 81

Section IV

The Psychic Being and Sadhana

Three Steps of Self-Realisation and the Triple Transformation	... 103
Becoming Conscious of the Psychic Being — Need for Sadhana	... 105
The Psychic Being and Conversion	... 107
Psychic Change — First Necessity	... 109
Emergence of the Psychic — Bringing Forward the Psychic	... 111
The Sunlit Way of the Psychic	... 122

Section V

The Afterlife and Rebirth

The Process of Rebirth	... 129
What Survives after Death and Reincarnates	... 134
The Psychic's Choice and Conditions of Rebirth	... 137
Memory of Past Lives	... 151

Section VI

More Lights on the Psychic Being	... 161
Glossary	... 201
References	... 214
Selected Bibliography	... 217
Index	... 218

PREFACE

The present compilation is an attempt to bring together in one volume the manifold teachings pertaining to the psychic being which are to be found in the numerous works of Sri Aurobindo and the Mother. The selections deal with the nature of the psychic being, shedding the light of Sri Aurobindo and the Mother on the inner constitution of the human being and on various related questions such as the process of inner growth, the after-life, rebirth, Sadhana or spiritual self-training, etc. Though the compilation is comprehensive, covering all the basic aspects of the subject-matter, it is not meant to be exhaustive. Being intended mainly for the general reader, it leaves out a good deal that would be of interest only to practitioners of Sri Aurobindo's yoga or to students of philosophy and philosophical psychology. The Selected Bibliography at the end of the book lists the major distinct sources where the interested reader will find additional material pertaining to the nature of the psychic being and its role in Sri Aurobindo's yoga.

In order to facilitate understanding, all the selections, except those in the last section of the book, have been classified into captioned sections and sub-sections, each dealing with a specific aspect of the subject-matter. However, since the book is a compilation from diverse sources, there is some overlapping as well as repetition in its contents. In order to maintain the wholeness and integrity of the extract, editing in the form of deleting statements within an extract or splitting a passage into several parts to fit the classification has been avoided. For the same reason, parenthetical remarks and statements pertaining to a topic other than the main theme of an extract, often found in Sri Aurobindo's letters and the Mother's answers to questions, have generally been retained.

The reason why Sri Aurobindo adopted the term "psychic being" has been stated by him as follows:

> "The word soul is very vaguely used in English — as it often refers to the whole non-physical consciousness including even the vital with all its desires and passions. That is why the word psychic being has to be used so as to distinguish this divine portion from the instrumental parts of the nature."*

The word "psychic" too, as Sri Aurobindo points out, has been used in a confused manner. Therefore the first section of the compilation contains extracts which deal with the various meanings of the words "soul" and "psychic", and clarify their connotations in Sri Aurobindo's yoga. To avoid confusion to those who might read some of Sri Aurobindo's earlier writings, particularly the unrevised parts of *The Synthesis of Yoga*, it may be pointed out that Sri Aurobindo had at first used the terms "psychic" and "psychical" interchangeably in referring to the occult phenomena. He also used the term "psychic" in such expressions as "psychic Prana" (as distinguished from physical Prana) and "psychic soul" (as distinguished from the desire-soul) to distinguish what is deeper or below the surface from that which is more on the surface. However, in the revised parts of the earlier writings and in

---

* *Letters on Yoga*, Sri Aurobindo Birth Centenary Library (Pondicherry, Sri Aurobindo Ashram, 1975), Vol. 22, p. 290.

Preface

later writings, he always used the term "psychic" to refer to the soul or inmost part of the being, which from the very beginning he called the psyche.

One of the most important points to be grasped clearly is the vital distinction between the soul *in its essence* — referred to variously by Sri Aurobindo as the psyche, psychic essence, psychic entity, psychic existence, soul-spark or soul element — and the soul *in its evolved, individualised form*, called the psychic being, psychic personality, soul-form, or soul-personality, which, in Sri Aurobindo's words, is "the spark growing into a fire, evolving with the growth of consciousness".* It should also be pointed out that the terms "soul" and "the psychic", when used without an epithet, sometimes refer to the soul-spark or psychic essence and sometimes to the soul-personality or psychic being.

The nature and function of the psychic being cannot be well explained without reference to other parts of the being. Therefore, the reader will find in this compilation frequent mention of the different parts of the being, several of which are designated by special terms in Sri Aurobindo's yoga. The Glossary at the end of the book includes these key terms in addition to Sanskrit terms as well as common English terms used in a special sense in Integral Yoga. It should be noted that some of the Sanskrit terms have a wider connotation than what is stated in the Glossary, and may have a different meaning in other contexts.

PUBLISHERS

---

* *Letters on Yoga*, Sri Aurobindo Birth Centenary Library (Pondicherry, Sri Aurobindo Ashram, 1975), Vol. 22, p. 278.

Section I

MEANING AND NATURE OF THE PSYCHIC BEING

This bodily appearance is not all;
The form deceives, the person is a mask;
Hid deep in man celestial powers can dwell.
His fragile ship conveys through the sea of years
An incognito of the Imperishable.
A spirit that is a flame of God abides,
A fiery portion of the Wonderful,
Artist of his own beauty and delight,
Immortal in our mortal poverty.
This sculptor of the forms of the Infinite,
This screened unrecognised Inhabitant,
Initiate of his own veiled mysteries,
Hides in a small dumb seed his cosmic thought.
In the mute strength of the occult Idea
Determining predestined shape and act,
Passenger from life to life, from scale to scale,
Changing his imaged self from form to form,
He regards the icon growing by his gaze
And in the worm foresees the coming god.

> Sri Aurobindo
> *Savitri*, Book I, Canto III

What is Meant by the Psychic Being

I mean by the psychic the inmost soul-being and the soul-nature. This is not the sense in which the word is used in ordinary parlance, or rather, if it is so used, it is with great vagueness and much-misprision of the true nature of this soul and it is given a wide extension of meaning which carries it far beyond that province. All phenomena of an abnormal or supernormal psychological or an occult character are dubbed psychic; if a man has a double personality changing from one to another, if an apparition of a dying man, something of his mere vital sheath or else a thought form of him, appears and stalks through the room of his wondering friend, if a poltergeist kicks up an unseemly row in a house, all that is classed under psychic phenomena and regarded as a fit object for psychic research, though these things have nothing whatever to do with the psychic. Again much in Yoga itself that is merely occult, phenomena of the unseen vital or mental or subtle physical planes, visions, symbols, all that mixed, often perturbed, often shadowy, often illusory range of experiences which belong to this intervening country between the soul and its superficial instruments, or rather to its outermost fringes, all the chaos of the intermediate zone, is summed up as psychic and considered as an inferior and dubious province of spiritual discovery. Again there is a constant confusion between the mentalised desire-soul which is a creation of the vital urge in man, of his life-force seeking for its fulfilment and the true soul which is a spark of the Divine Fire, a portion of the Divine. Because the soul, the psychic being uses the mind and the vital as well as the body as instruments for growth and experience it is itself looked at as if it were some amalgam or some subtle substratum of mind and life. But in Yoga if we accept all this chaotic mass as soul-stuff or soul-movement we shall enter into a confusion without an issue. All that belongs only to the coverings of the soul; the soul itself is an inner divinity greater than mind or life or body. It is something that once it is released from obscuration by its instruments at once creates a direct contact with the Divine and with the self and spirit.

SRI AUROBINDO

What is meant in the terminology of the yoga by the psychic is the soul element in the nature, the pure psyche or divine nucleus which stands behind mind, life and body (it is not the ego) but of which we are only dimly aware. It is a portion of the Divine and permanent from life to life, taking the experience of life through its outer instruments. As this experience grows it manifests a developing psychic personality which insisting always on the good, true and beautiful, finally becomes ready and strong enough to turn the nature towards the Divine. It can then come entirely forward, breaking through the mental, vital and physical screen, govern the instincts and transform the nature. Nature no longer imposes itself on the soul, but the soul, the Purusha, imposes its dictates on the nature.

SRI AUROBINDO

People do not understand what I mean by the psychic being, because the word psychic has been used in English to mean anything of the inner mental, inner vital or inner physical or anything abnormal or occult or even the more subtle movements of the outer being, all in a jumble; also occult phenomena are often called psychic. The distinction between these different parts of the being is unknown. Even in India the old knowledge of the Upanishads in which they are distinguished has been lost. The Jivatman, the psychic being (Purusha Antaratman), the Manomaya Purusha, the Pranamaya Purusha are all confused together.

SRI AUROBINDO

The psychic part of us is something that comes direct from the Divine and is in touch with the Divine. In its origin it is the nucleus pregnant with the divine possibilities that supports this lower triple manifestation of mind, life and body. There is this divine element in all living beings, but it stands hidden behind the ordinary consciousness, is not at first developed and, even when developed, is not always or often in the front; it expresses itself, so far as the imperfection of the instruments allows, by their means and under their limitations. It grows in the consciousness by Godward experience, gaining strength every time there is a higher movement in us, and, finally, by the accumulation of these deeper and higher movements, there is developed a psychic individuality, — that which we call usually the psychic being. It is always this psychic being that is the real, though often the secret cause of man's turning to the spiritual life and his greatest help in it. It is therefore that which we have to bring from behind to the front in the yoga.

The word 'soul', as also the word 'psychic', is used very vaguely and in many different senses in the English language.

More often than not, in ordinary parlance, no clear distinction is made between mind and soul and often there is an even more serious confusion, for the vital being of desire — the false soul or desire-soul — is intended by the words 'soul' and 'psychic' and not the true soul, the psychic being. The psychic being is quite different from the mind or vital; it stands behind them where they meet in the heart. Its central place is there, but behind the heart rather than in the heart; for what men call usually the heart is the seat of emotion, and human emotions are mental-vital impulses, not ordinarily psychic in their nature. This mostly secret power behind, other than the mind and the life-force, is the true soul, the psychic being in us. The power of the psychic, however, can act upon the mind and vital and body, purifying thought and perception and emotion (which then becomes psychic feeling) and sensation and action and everything else in us and preparing them to be divine movements.

The psychic being may be described in Indian language as the Purusha in the heart or the Chaitya Purusha;* but the

---

* The Chitta and the psychic part are not in the least the same. Chitta is a term in a quite different category in which are co-ordinated and put into their place the main functionings of our external consciousness, and to know it we need not go behind our surface or external nature.

'Category' means here another class of psychological factors, *tattva vibhāga*. The psychic belongs to one class — supermind, mind, life, psychic, physical — and covers both the inner and the outer nature. Chitta belongs to quite another class or category — buddhi, manas, chitta, prana, etc. — which is the classification made by ordinary Indian psychology; it covers only the psychology of the external being. In this category it is the main functions of our external consciousness only that are co-ordinated

Meaning and Nature of the Psychic Being

inner or secret heart must be understood, *hṛdaye guhāyām*, not the outer vital-emotional centre.

SRI AUROBINDO

Ordinarily, all the more inward and all the abnormal psychological experiences are called psychic. I use the word psychic for the soul as distinguished from the mind and vital. All movements and experiences of the soul would in that sense be called psychic, those which rise from or directly touch the psychic being; where mind and vital predominate, the experience would be called psychological (surface or occult).

SRI AUROBINDO

The word soul has various meanings according to the context; it may mean the Purusha supporting the formation of Prakriti, which we call a being, though the proper word would be rather a becoming; it may mean, on the other hand, specifically the psychic being in an evolutionary creature like man; it may mean the spark of the Divine which has been put into Matter by the descent of the Divine into the material world and which upholds all evolving formations here. There is and can be no psychic being in a non-evolutionary creature like the Asura; there can be none in a god who does not need one for his existence.

But what the god has is a Purusha and a Prakriti or Energy

---

and put in their place by the Indian thinkers; chitta is one of these main functions of the external consciousness and, therefore, to know it we need not go behind the external nature. [Sri Aurobindo's footnote] of nature of that Purusha. If any being of the typal worlds wants to evolve, he has to come down to earth and take a human body and accept to share in the evolution. It is because they do not want to do this that the vital beings try to possess men so that they may enjoy the materialities of physical life without having the burden of the evolution or the process of conversion in which it culminates.

SRI AUROBINDO

What exactly is the soul or psychic being? And what is meant by the evolution of the psychic being? What is its relation to the Supreme?

The soul and the psychic being are not exactly the same thing, although their essence is the same.

The soul is the divine spark that dwells at the centre of each being; it is identical with its Divine Origin; it is the divine in man.

The psychic being is formed progressively around this divine centre, the soul, in the course of its innumerable lives in the terrestrial evolution, until the time comes when the psychic being, fully formed and wholly awakened, becomes the conscious sheath of the soul around which it is formed.

And thus identified with the Divine, it becomes His perfect instrument in the world.

THE MOTHER

In the human being, is the psychic being the entire soul or do both the soul (in its essence as a divine spark in all creatures) and the psychic being exist together?

Meaning and Nature of the Psychic Being

The soul is the eternal essence at the centre of the psychic being. The soul is in fact like a divine spark which puts on many states of being of increasing density, down to the most material; it is inside the body, within the solar plexus, so to say.* These states of being take form and develop, progress, become individualised and perfected in the course of many earthly lives and form the psychic being. When the psychic being is fully formed, it is aware of the consciousness of the soul and manifests it perfectly.

THE MOTHER

Are the soul and the psychic being one and the same thing?

That depends on the definition you give to the words. In most religions, and perhaps in most philosophies also, it is the vital being which is called "soul", for it is said that "the soul leaves the body", while it is the vital being which leaves the body. One speaks of "saving the soul", "wicked souls", "redeeming the soul"... but all that applies to the vital being, for the psychic being has no need to be saved! It does not share the faults of the external person, it is free from all reaction.

THE MOTHER

A distinction has to be made between the soul in its essence

---

* By "solar plexus", the Mother is referring to the heart (not the navel) region; this is clear from statements she has made elsewhere; as for example, in the following statement: "Generally it is in the heart, behind the solar plexus, that one finds this luminous presence." (*Collected Works of the Mother*, Vol. 16, p. 410). See also the answer to the question, "Is the psychic being in the heart?" (p. 162)

and the psychic being. Behind each and all there is the soul which is the spark of the Divine — none could exist without that. But it is quite possible to have a vital and physical being without a clearly evolved psychic being behind it. Still, one cannot make general statements that no aboriginal has a soul or there is no display of soul anywhere.

The inner being is composed of the inner mental, inner vital, inner physical, — but that is not the psychic being. The psychic is the inmost being and quite distinct from these. The word 'psychic' is indeed used in English to indicate anything that is other or deeper than the external mind, life and body, anything occult or supraphysical, but that is a use which brings confusion and error and we entirely discard it when we speak or write about yoga. In ordinary parlance we may sometimes use the word 'psychic' in the looser popular sense or in poetry, which is not bound to intellectual accuracy, we may speak of the soul sometimes in the ordinary and more external sense or in the sense of the true psyche.

The psychic being is veiled by the surface movements and expresses itself as best it can through these outer instruments which are more governed by the outer forces than by the inner influences of the psychic. But that does not mean that they are entirely isolated from the soul. The soul is in the body in the same way as the mind or vital — but the body it occupies is not this gross physical frame only, but the subtle body also. When the gross sheath falls away, the vital and mental sheaths of the body still remain as the soul's vehicle till these too dissolve.

The soul of a plant or an animal is not altogether dormant — only its means of expression are less developed than those

Meaning and Nature of the Psychic Being

of a human being. There is much that is psychic in the plant, much that is psychic in the animal. The plant has only the vital-physical evolved in its form, so it cannot express itself; the animal has a vital mind and can, but its consciousness is limited and its experiences are limited, so the psychic essence has a less developed consciousness and experience than is present or at least possible in man. All the same, animals have a soul and can respond very readily to the psychic in man.

The ghost is of course not the soul. It is either the man appearing in his vital body or it is a fragment of his vital that is seized on by some vital force or being. The vital part of us normally exists after the dissolution of the body for some time and passes away into the vital plane where it remains till the vital sheath dissolves. Afterwards it passes, if it is mentally evolved, in the mental sheath to some mental world and finally the psychic leaves its mental sheath also and goes to its place of rest. If the mental is strongly developed, then the mental part of us can remain; so also can the vital, provided they are organised by and centred round the true psychic being — for they then share the immortality of the psychic. Otherwise the psychic draws mind and life into itself and enters into an internatal quiescence.

SRI AUROBINDO

In the experience of yoga the self or being is in essence one with the Divine or at least it is a portion of the Divine and has all the divine potentialities. But in manifestation it takes two aspects, the Purusha and Prakriti, conscious being and Nature. In Nature here the Divine is veiled, and the individual being is subjected to Nature which acts here as the lower Prakriti, a force of Ignorance, Avidya. The Purusha in itself is divine, but exteriorised in the ignorance of Nature it is the individual apparent being imperfect with her imperfection. Thus the soul or psychic essence, which is the Purusha entering into the evolution and supporting it, carries in itself all the divine potentialities; but the individual psychic being which it puts forth as its representative assumes the imperfection of Nature and evolves in it till it has recovered its full psychic essence and united itself with the Self above of which the soul is the individual projection in the evolution. This duality in the being on all its planes — for it is true in different ways not only of the Self and the psychic but of the mental, vital and physical Purushas — has to be grasped and accepted before the experiences of the yoga can be fully understood.

The Being is one throughout, but on each plane of Nature, it is represented by a form of itself which is proper to that plane, the mental Purusha in the mental plane, the vital Purusha in the vital, the physical Purusha in the physical. The Taittiriya Upanishad speaks of two other planes of the being, the Knowledge or Truth plane and the Ananda plane, each with its Purusha, but although influences may come down from them, these are superconscient to the human mind and their nature is not yet organised here.

Sri Aurobindo

Atman, Jivatman and the Psychic

It is necessary to understand clearly the difference between the evolving soul (psychic being) and the pure Atman, self or spirit. The pure self is unborn, does not pass through death or birth, is independent of birth or body, mind or life or this manifested Nature. It is not bound by these things, not limited, not affected, even though it assumes and supports them. The soul, on the contrary, is something that comes down into birth and passes through death — although it does not itself die, for it is immortal — from one state to another, from the earth plane to other planes and back again to the earth-existence. It goes on with this progression from life to life through an evolution which leads it up to the human state and evolves through it all a being of itself which we call the psychic being that supports the evolution and develops a physical, a vital, a mental human consciousness as its instruments of world-experience and of a disguised, imperfect, but growing self-expression. All this it does from behind a veil showing something of its divine self only in so far as the imperfection of the instrumental being will allow it. But a time comes when it is able to prepare to come out from behind the veil, to take command and turn all the instrumental nature towards a divine fulfilment. This is the beginning of the true spiritual life. The soul is able now to make itself ready for a higher evolution of manifested consciousness than the mental human — it can pass from the mental to the spiritual and through degrees of the spiritual to the supramental state. Till then there is no reason why it should cease from birth, it cannot in fact do so. If having reached the spiritual state, it wills to pass out of the terrestrial manifestation, it may indeed do so — but there is also possible a higher manifestation, in the Knowledge and not in the Ignorance.

SRI AUROBINDO

The phrase "central being" in our yoga is usually applied to the portion of the Divine in us which supports all the rest and survives through death and birth. This central being has two forms — above it is Jivatman, our true being, of which we become aware when the higher self-knowledge comes, — below, it is the psychic being which stands behind mind, body and life. The Jivatman is above the manifestation in life and presides over it; the psychic being stands behind the manifestation in life and supports it.

The natural attitude of the psychic being is to feel itself as the Child, the Son of God, the Bhakta; it is a portion of the Divine, one in essence, but in the dynamics of the manifestation there is always even in identity a difference. The Jivatman, on the contrary, lives in the essence and can merge itself in identity with the Divine; but it too, the moment it presides over the dynamics of the manifestation, knows itself as one centre of the multiple Divine, not as the Parameshwara. It is important to remember the distinction; for, otherwise, if there is the least vital egoism, one may begin to think of oneself as an Avatar or lose balance like Hridaya with Ramakrishna.

SRI AUROBINDO

The Spirit is the Atman, Brahman, Essential Divine.

When the One Divine manifests its ever inherent multiplicity, this essential Self or Atman becomes for that mani-

Meaning and Nature of the Psychic Being

festation the central being who presides from above over the evolution of its personalities and terrestrial lives here, but is itself an eternal portion of the Divine and prior to the terrestrial manifestation — *parā prakṛtir jīvabhūtā*.

In this lower manifestation, *aparā prakṛti*, this eternal portion of the divine appears as the soul, a spark of the Divine Fire, supporting the individual evolution, supporting the mental, vital and physical being. The psychic being is the spark growing into a Fire, evolving with the growth of the consciousness. The psychic being is therefore evolutionary, not like the Jivatman prior to the evolution.

But man is not aware of the self or Jivatman, he is aware only of his ego, or he is aware of the mental being which controls the life and the body. But more deeply he becomes aware of his soul or psychic being as his true centre, the Purusha in the heart; the psychic is the central being in the evolution, it proceeds from and represents the Jivatman, the eternal portion of the Divine. When there is the full consciousness, the Jivatman and the psychic being join together.

Sri Aurobindo

The soul, representative of the central being, is a spark of the Divine supporting all individual existence in Nature; the psychic being is a conscious form of that soul growing in the evolution — in the persistent process that develops first life in Matter, mind in life, until finally mind can develop into overmind and overmind into the supramental Truth. The soul supports the nature in its evolution through these grades, but is itself not any of these things.

The lower Nature, *aparā prakṛti*, is this external objective and superficial subjective apparent Nature which manifests all these minds, lives and bodies. The supreme Nature, *parā prakṛti*, concealed behind it is the very nature of the Divine — a supreme Consciousness-Force which manifests the multiple Divine as the Many. These Many are in themselves eternal selves of the Supreme in his supreme Nature, *parā prakṛti*. Here in relation to this world they appear as the Jivatmas supporting the evolution of the natural existences, *sarva-bhūtāni*, in the mutable Becoming which is the life of the Kshara (mobile or mutable) Purusha. The Jiva (or Jivatma) and the creatures, *sarva-bhūtāni*, are not the same thing. The Jivatmas really stand above the creation even though concerned in it; the natural existences, *sarva-bhūtāni*, are the creatures of Nature. Man, bird, beast, reptile are natural existences, but the individual Self in them is not even for a moment characteristically man, bird, beast or reptile; in its evolution it is the same through all these changes, a spiritual being that consents to the play of Nature.

What is original and eternal for ever in the Divine is the Being, what is developed in consciousness, conditions, forces, forms, etc. by the Divine Power is the Becoming. The eternal Divine is the Being; the universe in Time and all that is apparent in it is a Becoming. The eternal Being in its superior nature, Para Prakriti, is at once One and Many; but the eternal Multiplicity of the Divine when it stands behind the created existences, *sarva-bhūtāni*, appears as (or as we say, becomes) the Jiva, *parā prakṛtir jīvabhūtā*. In the psychic, on the other hand, there are two aspects, the psychic existence or soul behind and in front the form of individuality it takes in its evolution in Nature.

Meaning and Nature of the Psychic Being 17

The soul or psyche is immutable only in the sense that it contains all the possibilities of the Divine within it, but it has to evolve them and in its evolution it assumes the form of a developing psychic individual evolving in the manifestation the individual Prakriti and taking part in the evolution. It is the spark of the Divine Fire that grows behind the mind, vital and physical by means of the psychic being until it is able to transform the Prakriti of Ignorance into a Prakriti of Knowledge. This evolving psychic being is not therefore at any time all that the soul or essential psychic existence bears within it; it temporalises and individualises what is eternal in potentiality, transcendent in essence, in this projection of the spirit.

The central being is the being which presides over the different births one after the other, but is itself unborn, for it does not descend into the being but is above it — it holds together the mental, vital and physical being and all the various parts of the personality and it controls the life either through the mental being and the mental thought and will or through the psychic, whichever may happen to be most in front or most powerful in nature. If it does not exercise its control, then the consciousness is in great disorder and every part of the personality acts for itself so that there is no coherence in the thought, feeling or action.

The psychic is not above but behind — its seat is behind the heart, its power is not knowledge but an essential or spiritual feeling — it has the clearest sense of the Truth and a sort of inherent perception of it which is of the nature of soul-perception and soul-feeling. It is our inmost being and supports all the others, mental, vital, physical, but it is also much veiled by them and has to act upon them as an influence rather than by its sovereign right of direct action; its direct action becomes normal and preponderant only at a high stage of development or by yoga. It is not the psychic being which, you feel, gives you the intuitions of things to be or warns you against the results of certain actions; that is some part of the inner being, sometimes the inner mental, sometimes the inner vital, sometimes, it may be, the inner or subtle physical Purusha. The inner being — inner mind, inner vital, inner or subtle physical — knows much that is unknown to the outer mind, the outer vital, the outer physical, for it is in a more direct contact with the secret forces of Nature. The psychic is the inmost being of all; a perception of truth which is inherent in the deepest substance of the consciousness, a sense of the good, true, beautiful, the Divine, is its privilege.

The central being — the Jivatman which is not born nor evolves but presides over the individual birth and evolution — puts forward a representative of himself on each plane of the consciousness. On the mental plane it is the true mental being, *manomaya puruṣa*, on the vital plane the true vital being, *prāṇamaya puruṣa*, on the physical plane the true physical being, *annamaya puruṣa*. Each being, therefore is, so long as the Ignorance lasts, centred round his mental, vital or physical Purusha, according to the plane on which he predominantly lives, and that is to him his central being. But the true representative all the time is concealed behind the mind, vital and physical — it is the psychic, our inmost being.

When the inmost knowledge begins to come, we become aware of the psychic being within us and it comes forward and leads the sadhana. We become aware also of the Jivatman, the undivided Self or Spirit above the manifestation of which

Meaning and Nature of the Psychic Being

the psychic is the representative here.

SRI AUROBINDO

The Jivatman, spark-soul and psychic being are three different forms of the same reality and they must not be mixed up together, as that confuses the clearness of the inner experience.

The Jivatman or spirit, as it is usually called in English, is self-existent above the manifested or instrumental being — it is superior to birth and death, always the same, the individual Self or Atman. It is the eternal true being of the individual.

The soul is a spark of the Divine which is not seated above the manifested being, but comes down into the manifestation to support its evolution in the material world. It is at first an undifferentiated power of the Divine Consciousness containing all possibilities which have not yet taken form, but to which it is the function of evolution to give form. This spark is there in all living beings from the lowest to the highest.

The psychic being is formed by the soul in its evolution. It supports the mind, vital, body, grows by their experiences, carries the nature from life to life. It is the psychic or *chaitya puruṣa*. At first it is veiled by mind, vital and body, but as it grows, it becomes capable of coming forward and dominating the mind, life and body; in the ordinary man it depends on them for expression and is not able to take them up and freely use them. The life of the being is animal or human and not divine. When the psychic being can by sadhana become dominant and freely use its instruments, then the impulse towards the Divine becomes complete and the transformation of mind, vital and body, not merely their liberation, becomes possible.

The Self of Atman being free and superior to birth and death, the experience of the Jivatman and its unity with the supreme or universal Self brings the sense of liberation, it is this which is necessary for the supreme spiritual deliverance: but for the transformation of the life and nature the awakening of the psychic being and its rule over the nature are indispensable.

The psychic being realises its oneness with the true being, the Jivatman, but it does not change into it.

The *bindu* seen above may be a symbolic way of seeing the Jivatman, the portion of the Divine; the aspiration there would naturally be for the opening of the higher consciousness so that the being may dwell there and not in the Ignorance. The Jivatman is already one with the Divine in reality, but what is needed is that the rest of the consciousness should realise it.

The aspiration of the psychic being is for the opening of the whole lower nature, mind, vital, body to the Divine, for the love and union with Divine, for its presence and power within the heart, for the transformation of the mind, life and body by the descent of the higher consciousness into this instrumental being and nature.

Both aspirations are essential and indispensable for the fullness of this yoga. When the psychic imposes its aspiration on the mind, vital and body, then they too aspire and this is what was felt as the aspiration from the level of the lower being. The aspiration felt above is that of the Jivatman for the higher consciousness with its realisation of the One to manifest in the being. Therefore both aspirations help each other. The seeking of the lower being is necessarily at first intermittent and oppressed by the ordinary consciousness. It has, by sadhana, to become clear, constant, strong and enduring.

SRI AUROBINDO

Psychic-Mental, Psychic-Vital, Psychic-Physical

There is always a part of the mind, of the vital, of the body which is or can be influenced by the psychic; they can be called the psychic-mental, the psychic-vital, the psychic-physical. According to the personality or the degree of evolution of each person, this part can be small or large, weak or strong, covered up and inactive or prominent and in action. When it acts the movements of the mind, vital or physical accept the psychic motives or aims, partake of the nature of the psychic or follow its aims but with a modification in the manner which belongs to the mind, vital or physical. The psychic-vital seeks after the Divine, but it has a demand in its self-giving, desire, vital eagerness. The psychic has not, for the psychic has instead pure self-giving, aspiration, intensity of psychic fire. The psychic-vital is subject to pain and suffering, which there is not in the psychic.

SRI AUROBINDO

People mean different things when they speak of the soul. Sometimes it is what I have called in the *Arya* the desire-soul,— that is the vital with its mixed aspirations, desires, hungers of all kinds good and bad, its emotions, finer and grosser, or sensational urges crossed by the mind's idealisings and psychic stresses. But sometimes it is also the mind and vital under the stress of a psychic urge. The psychic, so long as it is veiled, must express itself through the mind and vital and its aspirations are mixed and coloured there by the vital and mental stuff. Thus the veiled psychic urge may express itself in the mind by a hunger in the thought for the knowledge of the Divine, what the Europeans call the intellectual love of God. In the vital it may express itself as a hunger or hankering after the Divine. It can bring much suffering because of the nature of the vital, its unquiet passions, desires, ardours, troubled emotions, cloudings, depressions, despairs. Nevertheless all cannot approach, at least cannot at once approach the Divine in the pure psychic way — the mental and vital approaches are often necessary beginnings and better from the spiritual point of view than unsensitiveness to the Divine. It is in both cases a call of the soul, the soul's urge — it only takes a form or colour due to the stress of the mind or vital nature.

Sri Aurobindo

Sweet Mother, here Sri Aurobindo has said: "If the inmost soul is awakened, if there is a new birth out of the mere mental, vital and physical into the psychic consciousness, then this Yoga can be done...". Why has he said "the inmost soul"? Is there a superficial soul?

It is because this inmost soul, that is, the central psychic being, influences the superficial parts of the consciousness (superficial in comparison with it: mental parts, vital parts).

Meaning and Nature of the Psychic Being 23

The purest mind, the highest vital, the emotive being — the soul influences them, influences them to an extent where one has the impression of entering into contact with it through these parts of the being. So people take these parts for the soul and that is why he says "the inmost soul", that is, the central soul, the real soul.

For very often, when one touches certain parts of the mind which are under the psychic influence and full of light and the joy of that light, or when one touches certain very pure and very high parts of the emotive being which has the most generous, most unselfish emotions, one also has the impression of being in contact with one's soul. But this is not the true soul, it is not the soul in its very essence. These are parts of the being under its influence and manifesting something of it. So, very often people enter into contact with these parts and this gives them illuminations, great joy, revelations, and they feel they have found their soul. But it is only the part of the being under its influence, one part or another, for... Exactly what happens is that one touches these things, has experiences, and then it gets veiled, and one wonders, "How is it that I touched my soul and now have fallen back into this state of ignorance and inconscience!" But that's because one had not touched one's soul, one had touched those parts of the being which are under the influence of the soul and manifest something of it, but are not it.

I have already said many times that when one enters consciously into contact with one's soul and the union is established, it is over, it can no longer be undone, it is something permanent, constant, which resists everything, and which, at any moment whatever, if referred to can be found; whereas the other things — one can have very fine experiences, and then it gets veiled again, and one tells oneself, "How does that happen? I saw my soul and now I don't find it any more!" It was not the soul one had seen. And these things are very beautiful and give you very impressive experiences, but this is not the contact with the psychic being itself.

The contact with the psychic being is definitive, and it is about this that I say, when people ask, "Do I have a contact with my psychic being?", "Your question itself proves that you don't have it!"

THE MOTHER

The Double Soul

There is a double soul or psychic term in us, as every other cosmic principle in us is also double. For we have two minds, one the surface mind of our expressed evolutionary ego, the superficial mentality created by us in our emergence out of Matter, another a subliminal mind which is not hampered by our actual mental life and its strict limitations, something large, powerful and luminous, the true mental being behind that superficial form of mental personality which we mistake for ourselves. So also we have two lives, one outer, involved in the physical body, bound by its past evolution in Matter, which lives and was born and will die, the other a subliminal force of life which is not cabined between the narrow boundaries of our physical birth and death, but is our true vital being behind the form of living which we ignorantly take for our real existence. Even in the matter of our being there is this duality; for behind our body we have a subtler material exist-

Meaning and Nature of the Psychic Being 25

ence which provides the substance not only of our physical but of our vital and mental sheaths and is therefore our real substance supporting this physical form which we erroneously imagine to be the whole body of our spirit. So too we have a double psychic entity in us, the surface desire-soul which works in our vital cravings, our emotions, aesthetic faculty and mental seeking for power, knowledge and happiness, and a subliminal psychic entity, a pure power of light, love, joy and refined essence of being which is our true soul behind the outer form of psychic existence we so often dignify by the name. It is when some reflection of this larger and purer psychic entity comes to the surface that we say of a man, he has a soul, and when it is absent in his outward psychic life that we say of him, he has no soul.

The external forms of our being are those of our small egoistic existence; the subliminal are the formations of our larger true individuality. Therefore are these that concealed part of our being in which our individuality is close to our universality, touches it, is in constant relation and commerce with it. The subliminal mind in us is open to the universal knowledge of the cosmic Mind, the subliminal life in us to the universal force of the cosmic Life, the subliminal physicality in us to the universal force-formation of cosmic Matter; the thick walls which divide from these things our surface mind, life, body and which Nature has to pierce with so much trouble, so imperfectly and by so many skilful-clumsy physical devices, are there, in the subliminal, only a rarefied medium at once of separation and communication. So too is the subliminal soul in us open to the universal delight which the cosmic soul takes in its own existence and in the existence of the myriad souls that represent it and in the operations of mind, life and matter by which Nature lends herself to their play and development; but from this cosmic delight the surface soul is shut off by egoistic walls of great thickness which have indeed gates of penetration, but in their entry through them the touches of the divine cosmic Delight become dwarfed, distorted or have to come in masked as their own opposites.

SRI AUROBINDO

The soul and the life are two quite different powers. The soul is a spark of the Divine Spirit which supports the individual nature; mind, life, body are the instruments for the manifestation of the nature. In most men the soul is hidden and covered over by the action of the external nature; they mistake the vital being for the soul, because it is the vital which animates and moves the body. But this vital being is a thing made up of desires and executive forces, good and bad; it is the desire-soul, not the true thing. It is when the true soul (psyche) comes forward and begins first to influence and then govern the actions of the instrumental nature that man begins to overcome vital desire and grow towards a divine nature.

SRI AUROBINDO

If knowledge is the widest power of the consciousness and its function is to free and illumine, yet love is the deepest and most intense and its privilege is to be the key to the most profound and secret recesses of the Divine Mystery. Man, because he is a mental being, is prone to give the highest importance to the thinking mind and its reason and will and

Meaning and Nature of the Psychic Being

to its way of approach and effectuation of Truth and, even, he is inclined to hold that there is no other. The heart with its emotions and incalculable movements is to the eye of his intellect an obscure, uncertain and often a perilous and misleading power which needs to be kept in control by the reason and the mental will and intelligence. And yet there is in the heart or behind it a profounder mystic light which, if not what we call intuition — for that, though not of the mind, yet descends through the mind — has yet a direct touch upon Truth and is nearer to the Divine than the human intellect in its pride of knowledge. According to the ancient teaching the seat of the immanent Divine, the hidden Purusha, is in the mystic heart, — the secret heart-cave *hṛdaye guhāyām*, as the Upanishads put it, — and, according to the experience of many Yogins, it is from its depths that there comes the voice or the breath of the inner oracle.

This ambiguity, these opposing appearances of depth and blindness are created by the double character of the human emotive being. For there is in front in men a heart of vital emotion similar to the animal's, if more variously developed; its emotions are governed by egoistic passion, blind instinctive affections and all the play of the life-impulses with their imperfections, perversions, often sordid degradations, — heart besieged and given over to the lusts, desires, wraths, intense or fierce demands or little greeds and mean pettinesses of an obscure and fallen life-force and debased by its slavery to any and every impulse. This mixture of the emotive heart and the sensational hungering vital creates in man a false soul of desire; it is this that is the crude and dangerous element which the reason rightly distrusts and feels a need to control, even though the actual control or rather coercion it succeeds in establishing over our raw and insistent vital nature remains always very uncertain and deceptive. But the true soul of man is not there; it is in the true invisible heart hidden in some luminous cave of the nature: there under some infiltration of the divine Light is our soul, a silent inmost being of which few are even aware; for if all have a soul, few are conscious of their true soul or feel its direct impulse. There dwells the little spark of the Divine which supports this obscure mass of our nature and around it grows the psychic being, the formed soul or the real Man within us. It is as this psychic being in him grows and the movements of the heart reflect its divinations and impulsions that man becomes more and more aware of his soul, ceases to be a superior animal, and, awakening to glimpses of the godhead within him, admits more and more its intimations of a deeper life and consciousness and an impulse towards things divine. It is one of the decisive moments of the integral Yoga when this psychic being liberated, brought out from the veil to the front, can pour the full flood of its divinations, seeings and impulsions on the mind, life and body of man and begin to prepare the upbuilding of divinity in the earthly nature.

SRI AUROBINDO

Nature of the Psychic Being

It is the very nature of the soul or the psychic being to turn towards the Divine Truth as the sunflower to the sun; it accepts and clings to all that is divine or progressing towards divinity and draws back from all that is a perversion or a

Meaning and Nature of the Psychic Being

denial of it, from all that is false and undivine. Yet the soul is at first but a spark and then a little flame of godhead burning in the midst of a great darkness; for the most part it is veiled in its inner sanctum and to reveal itself it has to call on the mind, the life-force and the physical consciousness and persuade them, as best they can, to express it; ordinarily, it succeeds at most in suffusing their outwardness with its inner light and modifying with its purifying fineness their dark obscurities or their coarser mixture. Even when there is a formed psychic being, able to express itself with some directness in life, it is still in all but a few a smaller portion of the being — "no bigger in the mass of the body than the thumb of a man" was the image used by the ancient seers — and it is not always able to prevail against the obscurity and ignorant smallness of the physical consciousness, the mistaken surenesses of the mind or the arrogance and vehemence of the vital nature. This soul is obliged to accept the human mental, emotive, sensational life as it is, its relations, its activities, its cherished forms and figures; it has to labour to disengage and increase the divine element in all this relative truth mixed with continual falsifying error, this love turned to the uses of the animal body or the satisfaction of the vital ego, this life of an average manhood shot with rare and pale glimpses of Godhead and the darker luridities of the demon and the brute. Unerring in the essence of its will, it is obliged often under the pressure of its instruments to submit to mistakes of action, wrong placement of feeling, wrong choice of person, errors in the exact form of its will, in the circumstances of its expression of the infallible inner ideal. Yet is there a divination within it which makes it a surer guide than the reason or than even the highest desire, and through apparent errors and stumblings its voice can still lead better than the precise intellect and the considering mental judgment. This voice of the soul is not what we call conscience — for that is only a mental and often conventional erring substitute; it is a deeper and more seldom heard call; yet to follow it when heard is wisest: even, it is better to wander at the call of one's soul than to go apparently straight with the reason and the outward moral mentor. But it is only when the life turns towards the Divine that the soul can truly come forward and impose its power on the outer members; for, itself a spark of the Divine, to grow in flame towards the Divine is its true life and its very reason of existence.

SRI AUROBINDO

The true soul secret in us, — subliminal, we have said, but the word is misleading, for this presence is not situated below the threshold of waking mind, but rather burns in the temple of the inmost heart behind the thick screen of an ignorant mind, life and body, not subliminal but behind the veil, — this veiled psychic entity is the flame of the Godhead always alight within us, inextinguishable even by that dense unconsciousness of any spiritual self within which obscures our outward nature. It is a flame born out of the Divine and, luminous inhabitant of the ignorance, grows in it till it is able to turn it towards the Knowledge. It is the concealed Witness and Control, the hidden Guide, the Daemon of Socrates, the inner light or inner voice of the mystic. It is that which endures and is imperishable in us from birth to birth, untouched by death, decay or corruption, an inde-

Meaning and Nature of the Psychic Being

structible spark of the Divine. Not the unborn Self or Atman, for the Self even in presiding over the existence of the individual is aware always of its universality and transcendence, it is yet its deputy in the forms of Nature, the individual soul, *caitya puruṣa*, supporting mind, life and body, standing behind the mental, the vital, the subtle-physical being in us and watching and profiting by their development and experience. These other person-powers in man, these beings of his being, are also veiled in their true entity, but they put forward temporary personalities which compose our outer individuality and whose combined superficial action and appearance of status we call ourselves: this inmost entity also, taking form in us as the psychic Person, puts forward a psychic personality which changes, grows, develops from life to life; for this is the traveller between birth and death and between death and birth, our nature parts are only its manifold and changing vesture. The psychic being can at first exercise only a concealed and partial and indirect action through the mind, the life and the body, since it is these parts of Nature that have to be developed as its instruments of self-expression, and it is long confined by their evolution. Missioned to lead man in the Ignorance towards the light of the Divine Consciousness, it takes the essence of all experience in the Ignorance to form a nucleus of soul-growth in the nature; the rest it turns into material for the future growth of the instruments which it has to use until they are ready to be a luminous instrumentation of the Divine. It is this secret psychic entity which is the true original Conscience in us deeper than the constructed and conventional conscience of the moralist, for it is this which points always towards Truth and Right and Beauty, towards Love and Harmony and all that is a divine possibility in us, and persists till these things become the major need of our nature. It is the psychic personality in us that flowers as the saint, the sage, the seer; when it reaches its full strength, it turns the being towards the Knowledge of Self and the Divine, towards the supreme Truth, the supreme Good, the supreme Beauty, Love and Bliss, the divine heights and largenesses, and opens us to the touch of spiritual sympathy, universality, oneness. On the contrary, where the psychic personality is weak, crude or ill-developed, the finer parts and movements in us are lacking or poor in character and power, even though the mind may be forceful and brilliant, the heart of vital emotions hard and strong and masterful, the life-force dominant and successful, the bodily existence rich and fortunate and an apparent lord and victor. It is then the outer desire-soul, the pseudo-psychic entity, that reigns and we mistake its misinterpretations of psychic suggestion and aspiration, its ideas and ideals, its desires and yearnings for true soul-stuff and wealth of spiritual experience.* If the

---

* The word "psychic" in our ordinary parlance is more often used in reference to this desire-soul than to the true psychic. It is used still more loosely of psychological and other phenomena of an abnormal or supernormal character which are really connected with the inner mind, inner vital, subtle physical being subliminal in us and are not at all direct operations of the psyche. Even such phenomena as materialisation and dematerialisation are included, though, if established, they evidently are not soul-action and would not shed any light upon the nature or existence of the psychic entity, but would rather be an abnormal action of an occult subtle physical energy intervening in the ordinary status of the gross body of things, reducing it to its own subtle condition and again reconstituting it in the terms of gross matter.

Meaning and Nature of the Psychic Being

secret psychic Person can come forward into the front and, replacing the desire-soul, govern overtly and entirely and not only partially and from behind the veil this outer nature of mind, life and body, then these can be cast into soul images of what is true, right and beautiful and in the end the whole nature can be turned towards the real aim of life, the supreme victory, the ascent into spiritual existence.

SRI AUROBINDO

Sweet Mother,
Sri Aurobindo says that the voice of the ordinary conscience is not the voice of the soul. What is it then?

The voice of the ordinary conscience is an ethical voice, a moral voice which distinguishes between good and evil, encourages us to do good and forbids us to do evil. This voice is very useful in ordinary life, until one is able to become conscious of one's psychic being and allow oneself to be entirely guided by it — in other words, to rise above ordinary humanity, free oneself from all egoism and become a conscious instrument of the Divine Will. The soul itself, being a portion of the Divine, is above all moral and ethical notions; it bathes in the Divine Light and manifests it, but it can truly govern the whole being only when the ego has been dissolved.

THE MOTHER

At a certain stage in the Yoga when the mind is sufficiently quieted and no longer supports itself at every step on the sufficiency of its mental certitudes, when the vital has been steadied and subdued and is no longer constantly insistent on its own rash will, demand and desire, when the physical has been sufficiently altered not to bury altogether the inner flame under the mass of its outwardness, obscurity or inertia, an inmost being hidden within and felt only in its rare influences is able to come forward and illumine the rest and take up the lead of the Sadhana. Its character is a one-pointed orientation towards the Divine or the Highest, one-pointed and yet plastic in action and movement; it does not create a rigidity of direction like the one-pointed intellect or bigotry of the regnant idea or impulse like the one-pointed vital force; it is at every moment and with a supple sureness that it points the way to the Truth, automatically distinguishes the right step from the false, extricates the divine or Godward movement from the clinging mixture of the undivine. Its action is like a searchlight showing up all that has to be changed in the nature; it has in it a flame of will insistent on perfection, on an alchemic transmutation of all the inner and outer existence. It sees the divine essence everywhere but rejects the mere mask and the disguising figure. It insists on Truth, on will and strength and mastery, on Joy and Love and Beauty, but on a Truth of abiding Knowledge that surpasses the mere practical momentary truth of the Ignorance, on an inward joy and not on mere vital pleasure, — for it prefers rather a purifying suffering and sorrow to degrading satisfactions, — on love winged upward and not tied to the stake of egoistic craving or with its feet sunk in the mire, on beauty restored to its priesthood of interpretation of the Eternal, on strength and will and mastery as instruments not of the ego but of the Spirit. Its will is for the divinisation of life, the expression

Meaning and Nature of the Psychic Being

through it of a higher Truth, its dedication to the Divine and the Eternal.

SRI AUROBINDO

In everybody, is the psychic always pure or has it to be made pure?

It is always pure. But it is either more or less individualised and independent in its action. What is psychic in the being is always pure, by its very definition, for it is that part of the being which is in contact with the Divine and expresses the truth of the being. But this may be like a spark in the darkness of the being or it may be a being of light, conscious, fully formed and independent. There are all the gradations between the two.

Usually is it veiled?

It is the outer consciousness that is not in contact with it, for it is turned outwards instead of being turned inwards — for it lives amidst all the external noises and movements, in what it sees, what it does, what it says, instead of looking within, into the depths of the being and listening to the inner inspirations.

THE MOTHER

It is the action of the psychic being, not the being itself, that gets mixed with the mental, vital and physical disabilities because it has to use them to express what little of the true psychic feeling gets through the veil. It is by the heart's aspiration to the Divine that the psychic being gets free from these disabilities.

SRI AUROBINDO

The soul is always pure, but the knowledge and force in it are involved and come out only as the psychic being evolves and grows stronger.

SRI AUROBINDO

Sweet Mother,
Does an outer life of evil deeds and a base consciousness have an effect on the psychic being? Is there a possibility of its degradation?

A base and evil life can only have the effect of separating the outer being more and more completely from the psychic being, which retires into the depths of the higher consciousness and sometimes even cuts off all relation with the body, which is then usually possessed by an asuric or rakshasic being.

The psychic being itself is above all possibility of degradation.

THE MOTHER

The Psychic and the Spiritual

Is there a difference between the "spiritual" and the "psychic"? Are they different planes?

Yes, the psychic plane belongs to the personal manifestation; the psychic is that which is divine in you put out to be dynamic in the play. But when we speak of the spiritual we are thinking of something that is concentrated in the Divine rather than in the external manifestation. The spiritual plane is something static behind and above the outward play; it supports the instruments of the nature, but is not itself included or involved in the external manifestation here.

But in speaking of these things one must be careful not to be imprisoned by the words we use. When I speak of the psychic or the spiritual, I mean things that are very deep and real behind the flat surface of the words and intimately connected even in their difference. Intellectual definitions and distinctions are too external and rigid to seize the true truth of things.

THE MOTHER

What is the difference between "spiritual" and "psychic"?

It is not the same thing. The psychic is the being organised by the divine Presence and it belongs to the earth — I am not speaking of the universe, only of the earth; it is only upon earth that you will find the psychic being. The rest of the universe is formed in quite a different way.

The universe contains all the domains higher than the physical: there is a global physical comprising the mental, the vital, etc., and all the domains above the mental are domains of a spiritual order, domains which are, for us, domains of the spirit, and it is this "spirit" which little by little, progressively, materialises itself to arrive at Matter as we conceive it. The beings of the Overmind, for instance, and all the beings of the higher regions have no psychic being —

the "angels" have no psychic being. It is only upon earth that the psychic life begins, and it is just the process by which the Divine has awakened material life to the necessity of rejoining its divine origin. Without the psychic, Matter would never have awakened from its inconscience, it would never have aspired for the life of its origin, the spiritual life. Therefore, the psychic being in the human being is the manifestation of spiritual aspiration; but there is a spiritual life independent of the psychic.

THE MOTHER

The psychic has two aspects — there is the soul principle itself which contains all soul possibilities and there is the psychic personality which represents whatever soul-power is developed from life to life or put forward for action in our present life-formation. The psychic being usually expresses itself through its instruments, mental, vital and physical; it tries to put as much of its own stamp on them as possible. But it can seldom put on them the full psychic stamp — unless it comes fully out from its rather secluded and overshadowed position and takes into its hands the direct government of the nature. It can then receive and express all spiritual realisations in its own way and manner. For the turn of the psychic is different from that of the overhead planes — it has less of greatness, power, wideness, more of a smaller sweetness, delicate beauty; there is an intense beauty of emotion, a fine subtlety of true perception, an intimate language. The expression "sweetness and light" can very well be applied to the psychic as the kernel of its nature. The spiritual plane, when it takes up these things, gives them a wider utterance, a

Meaning and Nature of the Psychic Being 39

greater splendour of light, a stronger sweetness, a breath of powerful audacity, strength and space.

SRI AUROBINDO

Emotion and Love — Vital and Psychic

Is an emotion always a vital movement?

It depends on the emotion and it also depends on what you call an emotion. For example, there is a state where, if you find yourself in the presence of a very precise, very clear psychic movement, a distinctly psychic movement — this happens quite often — the emotion is so powerful that tears come to your eyes. You are not sad, you are not happy, neither one nor the other; it doesn't correspond to any particular feeling, but it is an intensity of emotion which comes from something that is clearly, precisely psychic. It may be in yourself, but it is even more often in someone else. When you are in contact with an act, a movement, a manifestation which belongs to the psychic, then, all of a sudden, the eyes are filled with tears. If you call that an emotion... obviously it is an emotion. But usually, it comes from one thing: the physical being has a not very conscious but very intense longing for a contact with the psychic life. It feels poor, destitute, isolated and abandoned when it is not in contact with the psychic being. Not one physical being in a million is aware of this. But this kind of impression of being lost, left hanging, without protection, without support, of lacking something and not knowing what it is, something you don't understand but which you lack, an emptiness somewhere: well, this comes more often than one thinks — people have no idea what it is. But then, when for some reason or other this consciousness suddenly comes into contact with a clearly psychic phenomenon, with psychic forces, psychic vibrations, the feeling is so strong, so strong that certainly, most often, the body can hardly hold it. It is like a joy that is too great, that overflows on all sides, that you can't contain, can't hold in yourself. It is like that. There is suddenly a sort of revelation, not very conscious, not clearly expressed, the revelation of... this is it, this is what I must have. And it is so powerful, so powerful that it gives you an emotion, which is made up of so many things that you can hardly say what it is. These are emotions that are not vital.

Vital emotions are of an altogether different nature — they are very clear, very precise, you can express them very distinctly; they are violent, they usually fill you with an intensity, a restlessness, sometimes a great satisfaction. And then the opposite comes with the same force. And so people, many people think — we have mentioned this several times already — some people imagine they experience love only when it is like that, when love is in the vital, when it comes with all the movements of the vital, all this intensity, this violence, this precision, this glamour, this brightness. And when that is absent they say, "Oh, this is not love."

And yet that is exactly how love gets distorted: already it is no longer love, it is beginning to be passion. And this is an almost universal error among human beings.

Some people are full of a very pure, very high, very selfless psychic love and yet they know nothing about it and think they are cold, dry and without love because this admixture of vital vibration is absent. For them love begins

Meaning and Nature of the Psychic Being

and ends with this vibration.

And as it is something highly unstable which has movements and reactions and violences of all kinds, in depression as in satisfaction, love is something very ephemeral for these people: they have minutes of love in their lives. It may last a few hours and then it becomes dull and flat again and they imagine that love has deserted them.

As I said, some people are quite beyond that, they have been able to control it in such a way that it does not get mixed up with anything else; they have in themselves this psychic love which is full of self-forgetfulness, of self-giving, compassion, generosity, nobility of life, and is a great power of identification. So most of these people think they are cold or indifferent — they are very nice people, you see, but they do not love — and sometimes they themselves do not know. I have known people who thought they had no love because they didn't have this vital vibration. Usually, when people speak of emotions, they are speaking of vital emotions. But there is another kind of emotion which is of an infinitely higher order and doesn't express itself in the same way, which has just as much intensity, but an intensity that is under control, contained, condensed, concentrated, and is an extraordinary dynamic power.

True love can achieve extraordinary things, but it is rare. All kinds of miracles can be done out of love for the person one loves — not for everyone, but for the people or the person one loves. But it has to be a love free from all vital mixture, an absolutely pure and selfless love which demands nothing in return, which expects nothing in return.

THE MOTHER

It is also a mistake to think that the vital alone has warmth and the psychic is something frigid without any flame in it. A clear limpid goodwill is a very good and desirable thing. But that is not what is meant by psychic love. Love is love and not merely goodwill. Psychic love can have a warmth and a flame as intense and more intense than the vital, only it is a pure fire, not dependent on the satisfaction of ego-desire or on the eating up of the fuel it embraces. It is a white flame, not a red one; but white heat is not inferior to the red variety in its ardour. It is true that the psychic love does not usually get its full play in human relations and human nature; it finds the fullness of its fire and ecstasy more easily when it is lifted towards the Divine. In the human relation the psychic love gets mixed up with other elements which seek at once to use it and overshadow it. It gets an outlet for its own full intensities only at rare moments. Otherwise it comes in only as an element, but even so it contributes all the higher things in a love fundamentally vital — all the finer sweetness, tenderness, fidelity, self-giving, self-sacrifice, reachings of soul to soul, idealising sublimations that lift up human love beyond itself, come from the psychic. If it could dominate and govern and transmute the other elements, mental, vital, physical, of human love, then love could be on the earth some reflection or preparation of the real thing, an integral union of the soul and its instruments in a dual life. But even some imperfect appearance of that is rare.

SRI AUROBINDO

Knowledge — Mental and Psychic

The mental being within watches, observes and passes judgment on all that happens in you. The psychic does not watch and observe in this way like a witness, but it feels and knows spontaneously in a much more direct and luminous way, by the very purity of its own nature and the divine instinct within it, and so, whenever it comes to the front it reveals at once what are the right and what the wrong movements in your nature.

SRI AUROBINDO

Communications from the psychic do not come in a mental form. They are not ideas or reasonings. They have their own character quite distinct from the mind, something like a feeling that comprehends itself and acts.

By its very nature, the psychic is calm, quiet and luminous, understanding and generous, wide and progressive. Its constant effort is to understand and progress.

The mind describes and explains.

The psychic sees and understands.

THE MOTHER

One may have knowledge from the psychic — though it is of another kind and is not formulated as in the mind. It is a sort of inner certitude which makes you do the right thing at the right moment and in the right way, without necessarily passing through the reason or mental formation.

For instance, one may act with a perfect knowledge of what should be done, and without intervention — the least intervention — of the reasoning mind. The mind is silent: it simply looks on and listens in order to register things, it does not act.

THE MOTHER

The perception of the exterior consciousness may deny the perception of the psychic. But the psychic has the true knowledge, an intuitive instinctive knowledge. It says, "I know; I cannot give reasons, but I know." For its knowledge is not mental, based on experience or proved true. It does not believe after proofs are given: faith is the movement of the soul whose knowledge is spontaneous and direct. Even if the whole world denies and brings forward a thousand proofs to the contrary, still it knows by an inner knowledge, a direct perception that can stand against everything, a perception by identity. The knowledge of the psychic is something which is concrete and tangible, a solid mass. You can also bring it into your mental, your vital and your physical; and then you have an integral faith — a faith which can really move mountains. But nothing in the being must come and say "It is not like that", or ask for a test. By the least half-belief you spoil matters. How can the Supreme manifest if faith is not integral and immovable? Faith in itself is always unshakable — that is its very nature, for otherwise it is not faith at all. But it may happen that the mind or vital or the physical does not follow the psychic movement. A man can come to a Yogi and have a sudden faith that this person will lead him to his goal. He does not know whether the person has knowledge or not. He feels a psychic shock and knows that he has met his master. He does not believe after long mental consideration or

Meaning and Nature of the Psychic Being

seeing many miracles. And this is the only kind of faith worthwhile. You will always miss your destiny if you start arguing. Some people sit down and consider whether the psychic impulse is reasonable or not.

It is not really by what is called blind faith that people are misled. They often say, "Oh, I have believed in this or that man and he has betrayed me!" But in fact the fault lies not with the man but with the believer: it is some weakness in himself. If he had kept his faith intact he would have changed the man: it is because he did not remain in the same faith-consciousness that he found himself betrayed and did not make the man what he wanted him to be. If he had had integral faith, he would have obliged the man to change. It is always by faith that miracles happen. A person goes to another and has a contact with the Divine Presence; if he can keep this contact pure and sustained, it will oblige the Divine Consciousness to manifest in the most material. But all depends on your own standard and your own sincerity; and the more you are psychically ready the more you are led to the right source, the right master. The psychic and its faith are always sincere, but if in your exterior being there is insincerity and if you are seeking not spiritual life but personal powers, that can mislead you. It is that and not your faith that misleads you. Pure in itself, faith can get mixed up in the being with low movements and it is then that you are misled.

THE MOTHER

Section II

ROLE, FUNCTION AND ACTION OF THE PSYCHIC

This seed-self sown in the Indeterminate
Forfeits its glory of divinity,
Concealing the omnipotence of its Force,
Concealing the omniscience of its Soul;
An agent of its own transcendent Will,
It merges knowledge in the inconscient deep;
Accepting error, sorrow, death and pain,
It pays the ransom of the ignorant Night,
Redeeming by its substance Nature's fall.

Sri Aurobindo
Savitri, Book III, Canto III

In this investiture of fleshly life
A soul that is a spark of God survives
And sometimes it breaks through the sordid screen
And kindles a fire that makes us half-divine.

Ibid., Book II, Canto V

Our soul from its mysterious chamber acts;
Its influence pressing on our heart and mind
Pushes them to exceed their mortal selves.
It seeks for Good and Beauty and for God;
We see beyond self's walls our limitless self,
We gaze through our world's glass at half-seen vasts,
We hunt for the Truth behind apparent things.

Ibid., Book VII, Canto II

Function of the Psychic

This is the function of the psychic — it has to work on each plane so as to help each to awaken to the true truth and the Divine Reality.

SRI AUROBINDO

Is it the psychic will which wants the being to be identified with the Divine?

Yes, surely. It is the will of the psychic. It is also the very reason of its existence. It is for that it is there. For example, in the mind certain activities (and even at times in the physical and vital) ... awaken to the influence of the psychic without even knowing it. That is why those parts adhere to it and begin to aspire also for the divine knowledge, the divine union, the relation with the Divine.

THE MOTHER

What is the work of the psychic being?

What is the work of the psychic being? You want it to have some work? What do you want to say exactly? What is its function? Ah! Very well. One could put it this way, that it is like an electric wire that connects the generator with the lamp. Now, if someone has understood, let him explain what I said!

What is the generator and what the lamp? (Laughter)

Ah, there we are! So, what is the generator and what the lamp? That is exactly it. What is the generator and what the lamp? Or rather, who is the generator and who is the lamp?

The generator is the Divine and the lamp is the body.

It is the body, it is the visible being.

So, that is its function. This means that if there were no psychic in Matter, it would not be able to have any direct contact with the Divine. And it is happily due to this psychic presence in Matter that the contact between Matter and the Divine can be direct and all human beings can be told, "You carry the Divine within you, and you have only to enter within yourself and you will find Him." It is something very particular to the human being or rather to the inhabitants of the earth. In the human being the psychic becomes more conscious, more formed, more conscious and more independent also. It is individualised in human beings. But it is a speciality of the earth. It is a direct infusion, special and redeeming, in the most inconscient and obscure Matter, so that it might once again awake through stages to the divine Consciousness, the divine Presence and finally to the Divine Himself. It is the presence of the psychic which makes man an exceptional being — I don't like to tell him this very much, because already he thinks too much of himself; he has such a high opinion of himself that it is not necessary to encourage him! But still, this is a fact — so much so that there are beings of other domains of the universe, those called by some people demigods and even gods, beings, for instance, of what Sri Aurobindo calls the Overmind, who are very eager to take a physical body on earth to have the experience of the psychic, for they don't have it. These beings certainly have

Role, Function and Action of the Psychic

many qualities that men don't, but they lack this divine presence which is altogether exceptional and exists only on the earth and nowhere else. All these inhabitants of the higher worlds, the Higher Mind, Overmind and other regions have no psychic being. Of course, the beings of the vital worlds don't have it either. But these latter don't regret it, they don't want it. There are only those very rare ones, quite exceptional, who want to be converted, and for this they act without delay, they immediately take a physical body. The others don't want it; it is something which binds them and constrains them to a rule they do not want.

But it is a fact, so I am obliged to state that this is how it is, that it is an exceptional quality of the human being to carry within himself the psychic and, truly speaking, he does not take full advantage from it. He does not seem to consider this quality as something very, very desirable, from the way he treats this presence — exactly that! He prefers to it the ideas of his mind, prefers the desires of his vital being and the habits of his physical.

THE MOTHER

Sweet Mother,
  What is the role of the soul?

But without the soul we wouldn't exist!

The soul is that which comes from the Divine without ever leaving Him, and returns to the Divine without ceasing to be manifest.

The soul is the Divine made individual without ceasing to be divine.

In the soul the individual and the Divine are eternally one; therefore, to find one's soul is to find God; to identify with one's soul is to unite with the Divine.

Thus it may be said that the role of the soul is to make a true being of man.

THE MOTHER

Influence and Action of the Psychic

At the beginning the soul in Nature, the psychic entity, whose unfolding is the first step towards a spiritual change, is an entirely veiled part of us, although it is that by which we exist and persist as individual beings in Nature. The other parts of our natural composition are not only mutable but perishable; but the psychic entity in us persists and is fundamentally the same always: it contains all essential possibilities of our manifestation but is not constituted by them; it is not limited by what it manifests, not contained by the incomplete forms of the manifestation, not tarnished by the imperfections and impurities, the defects and depravations of the surface being. It is an ever-pure flame of the divinity in things and nothing that comes to it, nothing that enters into our experience can pollute its purity or extinguish the flame. This spiritual stuff is immaculate and luminous and, because it is perfectly luminous, it is immediately, intimately, directly aware of truth of being and truth of nature; it is deeply conscious of truth and good and beauty because truth and good and beauty are akin to its own native character, forms of something that is inherent in its own substance. It is aware also of all that contradicts these things, of all that deviates

Role, Function and Action of the Psychic 53

from its own native character, of falsehood and evil and the ugly and the unseemly; but it does not become these things nor is it touched or changed by these opposites of itself which so powerfully affect its outer instrumentation of mind, life and body. For the soul, the permanent being in us, puts forth and uses mind, life and body as its instruments, undergoes the envelopment of their conditions, but it is other and greater than its members.

If the psychic entity had been from the beginning unveiled and known to its ministers, not a secluded King in a screened chamber, the human evolution would have been a rapid soul-outflowering, not the difficult, chequered and disfigured development it now is; but the veil is thick and we know not the secret Light within us, the light in the hidden crypt of the heart's innermost sanctuary. Intimations rise to our surface from the psyche, but our mind does not detect their source; it takes them for its own activities because, before even they come to the surface, they are clothed in mental substance: thus ignorant of their authority, it follows or does not follow them according to its bent or turn at the moment. If the mind obeys the urge of the vital ego, then there is little chance of the psyche at all controlling the nature or manifesting in us something of its secret spiritual stuff and native movement; or, if the mind is over-confident to act in its own smaller light, attached to its own judgment, will and action of knowledge, then also the soul will remain veiled and quiescent and wait for the mind's farther evolution. For the psychic part within is there to support the natural evolution, and the first natural evolution must be the development of body, life and mind, successively, and these must act each in its own kind or together in their ill-assorted partnership in order to grow and have experience and evolve. The soul gathers the essence of all our mental, vital and bodily experience and assimilates it for the farther evolution of our existence in Nature; but this action is occult and not obtruded on the surface. In the early material and vital stages of the evolution of being there is indeed no consciousness of soul; there are psychic activities, but the instrumentation, the form of these activities are vital and physical, — or mental when the mind is active. For even the mind, so long as it is primitive or is developed but still too external, does not recognise their deeper character. It is easy to regard ourselves as physical beings or beings of life or mental beings using life and body and to ignore the existence of the soul altogether: for the only definite idea that we have of the soul is of something that survives the death of our bodies; but what this is we do not know because even if we are conscious sometimes of its presence, we are not normally conscious of its distinct reality nor do we feel clearly its direct action in our nature.

As the evolution proceeds, Nature begins slowly and tentatively to manifest our occult parts; she leads us to look more and more within ourselves or sets out to initiate more clearly recognisable intimations and formations of them on the surface. The soul in us, the psychic principle, has already begun to take secret form; it puts forward and develops a soul-personality, a distinct psychic being to represent it. This psychic being remains still behind the veil in our subliminal part, like the true mental, the true vital or the true or subtle physical being within us: but, like them, it acts on the surface life by the influences and intimations it throws up upon that surface; these form part of the surface aggregate which is the conglomerate effect of the inner influences and upsurgings, the visible formation and superstructure which we ordinarily experience and think of as ourselves. On this ignorant surface we become dimly aware of something that can be called a soul as distinct from mind, life or body; we feel it not only as our mental idea or vague instinct of ourselves, but as a sensible influence in our life and character and action. A certain sensitive feeling for all that is true and good and beautiful, fine and pure and noble, a response to it, a demand for it, a pressure on mind and life to accept and formulate it in our thought, feelings, conduct, character is the most usually recognised, the most general and characteristic, though not the sole sign of this influence of the psyche. Of the man who has not this element in him or does not respond at all to this urge, we say that he has no soul. For it is this influence that we can most easily recognise as a finer or even a diviner part in us and the most powerful for the slow turning towards some aim at perfection in our nature.

But this psychic influence or action does not come up to the surface quite pure or does not remain distinct in its purity; if it did, we would be able to distinguish clearly the soul element in us and follow consciously and fully its dictates. An occult mental and vital and subtle-physical action intervenes, mixes with it, tries to use it and turn it to its own profit, dwarfs its divinity, distorts or diminishes its self-expression, even causes it to deviate and stumble or stains it with the impurity, smallness and error of mind and life and body. After it reaches the surface, thus alloyed and diminished, it is taken hold of by the surface nature in an obscure reception and ignorant formation, and there is or can be by this cause a still further deviation and mixture. A twist is given, a wrong direction is imparted, a wrong application, a wrong formation, an erroneous result of what is in itself pure stuff and action of our spiritual being; a formation of consciousness is accordingly made which is a mixture of the psychic influence and its intimations jumbled with mental ideas and opinions, vital desires and urges, habitual physical tendencies. There coalesce too with the obscured soul-influence the ignorant though well-intentioned efforts of these external parts towards a higher direction; a mental ideation of a very mixed character, often obscure even in its idealism, sometimes even disastrously mistaken, a fervour and passion of the emotional being throwing up its spray and foam of feelings, sentiments, sentimentalisms, a dynamic enthusiasm of the life-parts, eager responses of the physical, the thrills and excitements of nerve and body, — all these influences coalesce in a composite formation which is frequently taken as the soul and its mixed and confused action for the soul-stir, for a psychic development and action or a realised inner influence. The psychic entity is itself free from stain or mixture, but what comes up from it is not protected by that immunity; therefore this confusion becomes possible.

Moreover, the psychic being, the soul-personality in us, does not emerge full-grown and luminous; it evolves, passes through a slow development and formation; its figure of being may be at first indistinct and may afterwards remain for a long time weak and undeveloped, not impure but imperfect: for it rests its formation, its dynamic self-building on

Role, Function and Action of the Psychic

the power of soul that has been actually and more or less successfully, against the resistance of the Ignorance and Inconscience, put forth in the evolution upon the surface. Its appearance is the sign of a soul-emergence in Nature, and if that emergence is as yet small and defective, the psychic personality also will be stunted or feeble. It is too, by the obscurity of our consciousness, separated from its inner reality, in imperfect communication with its own source in the depths of the being; for the road is as yet ill-built, easily obstructed, the wires often cut or crowded with communications of another kind and proceeding from another origin: its power to impress what it receives upon the outer instruments is also imperfect; in its penury it has for most things to rely on these instruments and it forms its push to expression and action on their data and not solely on the unerring perceptions of the psychic entity. In these conditions it cannot prevent the true psychic light from being diminished or distorted in the mind into a mere idea or opinion, the psychic feeling in the heart into a fallible emotion or mere sentiment, the psychic will to action in the life-parts into a blind vital enthusiasm or a fervid excitement: it even accepts these mistranslations for want of something better and tries to fulfil itself through them. For it is part of the work of the soul to influence mind and heart and vital being and turn their ideas, feelings, enthusiasms, dynamisms in the direction of what is divine and luminous; but this has to be done at first imperfectly, slowly and with a mixture. As the psychic personality grows stronger, it begins to increase its communion with the psychic entity behind it and improve its communications with the surface: it can transmit its intimations to the mind and heart and life with a greater purity and force; for it is more able to exercise a strong control and react against false mixture; now more and more it makes itself distinctly felt as a power in the nature. But even so this evolution would be slow and long if left solely to the difficult automatic action of the evolutionary Energy; it is only when man awakes to the knowledge of the soul and feels a need to bring it to the front and make it the master of his life and action that a quicker conscious method of evolution intervenes and a psychic transformation becomes possible.

SRI AUROBINDO

How does the soul influence a being who is normally unconscious?

The soul's influence is a kind of radiance that penetrates through the most opaque substances and acts even in the unconsciousness.

But then its action is slow and takes a very long time to obtain a perceptible result.

THE MOTHER

In the ordinary consciousness in which the mind etc. are *not* awakened the psychic acts as well as it can through them, but according to the laws of the Ignorance.

SRI AUROBINDO

The psychic being is there in all, but in very few is it well developed, well built up in the consciousness or prominent in the front; in most it is veiled, often ineffective or only an

Role, Function and Action of the Psychic

influence, not conscious enough or strong enough to support the spiritual life.

SRI AUROBINDO

What you describe is the psychic fire, *agni pāvaka*, which burns in the deeper heart and from there is lighted in the mind, the vital and the physical body. In the mind Agni creates a light of intuitive perception and discrimination which sees at once what is the true vision or idea and the wrong vision or idea, the true feeling and the wrong feeling, the true movement and the wrong movement. In the vital it is kindled as a fire of right emotion and a kind of intuitive feeling, a sort of tact which makes for the right impulse, the right action, the right sense of things and reaction to things. In the body it initiates a similar but still more automatic correct response to the things of physical life, sensation, body experience. Usually it is the psychic light in the mind that is first lit of the three, but not always — for sometimes it is the psycho-vital flame that takes precedence.

In ordinary life also there is no doubt an action of the psychic — without it man would be only a thinking and planning animal. But its action there is very much veiled, needing always the mental or vital to express it, usually mixed and not dominant, not unerring therefore; it does often the right thing in the wrong way, is moved by the right feeling but errs as to the application, person, place, circumstance. The psychic, except in a few extraordinary natures, does not get its full chance in the outer consciousness; it needs some kind of Yoga or Sadhana to come by its own and it is as it emerges more and more in front that it gets clear of the mixture. That is to say, its presence becomes directly felt, not only behind and supporting, but filling the frontal consciousness and no longer dependent or dominated by its instruments — mind, vital and body, but dominating them and moulding them into luminosity and teaching them their true action.

SRI AUROBINDO

Guidance through Organisation of Life

Has the psychic any power?

Power? It is usually the psychic which guides the being. One knows nothing about it because one is not conscious of it but usually it is that which guides the being. If one is very attentive, one becomes aware of it. But the majority of men haven't the least idea of it. For instance, when they have decided, in their outer ignorance, to do something, and instead of their being able to do it, all the circumstances are so organised that they do something else, they start shouting, storming, flying into a rage against fate, saying (that depends on what they believe, their beliefs) that Nature is wicked or their destiny baleful or God unjust, or... no matter what (it depends on what they believe). Whilst most of the time it is just the very circumstance which was most favourable for their inner development. And naturally, if you ask the psychic to help you to fashion a pleasant life for yourself, to earn money, have children who will be the pride of the family, etc., well, the psychic will not help you. But it will create for you all the circumstances necessary to awaken something in you so that the need of union with the Divine may

Role, Function and Action of the Psychic

be born in your consciousness. At times you have made fine plans, and if they had succeeded, you would have been more and more encrusted in your outer ignorance, your stupid little ambition and your aimless activity. Whilst if you receive a good shock, and the post you coveted is denied to you, the plan you made is shattered, and you find yourself completely thwarted, then, sometimes this opposition opens to you a door on something truer and deeper. And when you are a little awake and look back, if you are in the least sincere, you say: "Ah! It wasn't I who was right — it was Nature or the divine Grace or my psychic being who did it." It is the psychic being which organised that.

THE MOTHER

If you have within you a psychic being sufficiently awake to watch over you, to prepare your path, it can draw towards you things which help you, draw people, books, circumstances, all sorts of little coincidences which come to you as though brought by some benevolent will and give you an indication, a help, a support to take decisions and turn you in the right direction. But once you have taken this decision, once you have decided to find the truth of your being, once you start sincerely on the road, then everything seems to conspire to help you to advance.

THE MOTHER

When someone is destined for the Path, all circumstances through all the deviations of mind and life help in one way or another to lead him to it. It is his own psychic being within him and Divine Power above that use to that end the vicissitudes both of mind and outward circumstance.

SRI AUROBINDO

Some people say there is something outside their own will that organises their whole life, that puts them in the required condition, that attracts favourable circumstances or people, that arranges everything outside them, so to say. In their outer consciousness, perhaps they wanted something and worked for it, but something else came. Well, after some years, they realise that this is what really had to happen. You may know nothing of the existence of a psychic being within you and yet be guided by it. For, in order to become aware of something, you must first of all admit that this thing exists. Some people don't. I have known people who had a genuine contact with their psychic being without knowing at all what it was, because there was nothing in them that corresponded to the knowledge of this contact.

THE MOTHER

Mother, is the orientation of an individual's life directed by the psychic?

Yes. Absolutely unconsciously for the individual, most of the time; but it is the psychic which organises his existence — only in what may be called the main lines, because for intervening in the details there would have to be a conscious union between the outer being, that is, the vital being and physical being, and the psychic being, but usually this does not exist. So externally, in the details... for example, there was someone who in deep perplexity said to me, "Well, if it

Role, Function and Action of the Psychic 63

is the psychic being or rather the Divine in the psychic who directs our life, is it He who decides the number of pieces of sugar I put in my tea-cup?" That was the question, verbatim. So the answer had to be, "No, because it is not a detailed intervention of this kind."

It is as when you push your fist into a heap of iron filings or saw-dust, all the infinitesimal little elements of the iron filings or saw-dust are organised to take on the form of your fist, but they do not do this either deliberately or consciously. It is through the work of the consciousness which pushes that this kind of thing happens. There is no decision that each element is going to be exactly in this place, like that; it is the effect of the energy which has pushed the fist that organises the elements. But that's how it is. There is the psychic consciousness at work in life, organising all the circumstances of your life but not with a deliberate choice of the details; and in fact very few things are deliberate and conscious in the organisation of the physical life of human beings. Most of the time that's what happens. If you ask someone, "Why have you done this?" — "That's how it happened." It is always like that: "That's how it happened." At least seventy-five times out of a hundred. Only, one is so used to going, moving, and doing things like that that one doesn't even notice it. But if one begins to observe himself, he sees that it is true. There are very few things which were the result of a clear and willed decision, very few, only what one considers important things, and even here there is a wide margin. The amount of inconscience that's mixed with the physical consciousness is tremendous, but because we are used to it we do not notice it. But as soon as you begin to analyse, look, study, you are terrified. How many times you are just faced with a question. You see, you do things automatically, by habit, perhaps sometimes by choice — sometimes, but suddenly you find yourself facing an absolutely insignificant detail: "Should I do this or should I do that?" Simply this. You can take very small things like... you are in the course of eating, and you ask yourself, "Should I continue eating or should I stop?" How many times can you take a motivated and conscious decision? And you suddenly realise, "Why, I know nothing about it", and "I don't know; I can do this, I can do that; I can do that and that and that. But what will choose in me?" Unless you have mental constructions. But then if you have mental constructions ruling your life, you don't even ask yourself these questions, you live like an automaton, in a habitual routine you have made for yourself. But it's not just once, it happens a thousand times daily.

For example, you are in contact with someone, you have very good feelings for this person; you find yourself in a slightly difficult circumstance and want to do the best possible. If you act spontaneously, there is no problem before you because you act like that, one thing trailing another, and without reflecting. And you consciously want to do the best... On what will you base your judgment? What knowledge will allow you to decide: "I must do this or I must do that, I must say this or I must say that or I must not say anything" — all the countless possibilities which come before you? And on what will you base your judgment? If you look at it sincerely, you will find out that at each step you do not know.

It is only if you have been in the habit of going within yourself, of referring to the inner psychic consciousness and

Role, Function and Action of the Psychic

letting it decide in yourself what you want to do, that you do it with certitude, without hesitation, without a question, nothing. You know that this is what must be done and there is no question about it; but that's the only case. Therefore it is only when you let your psychic guide you consciously, constantly, that you are able to do consciously and constantly the right thing; but that's the only case.

In the other case, if you have made it a habit to study and observe, you have before you all the little things of life which recur constantly. You don't want to live mechanically by a kind of habit, you want to live consciously, making use of your will. Well, at every minute you are facing a problem which you can't solve, I mean purely physically. Take a certain difficulty you have in your body — what we call a disorder — which is expressed by an uneasiness or an indisposition; it is not an illness, it is an indisposition, it is an uneasiness, there is something that's not working very well. Then if you don't have the psychic knowledge which makes you directly do the thing which ought to be done and without any argument, if you want to refer the thing to your mind and to what you consider to be the knowledge you have, then... Take a case which lies in the field of medicine, that is, "Should I do this or that, take this medicine or that, change the diet, take this food or that?"... Then you look. If you have never known more than a certain number of very primary principles, your choice is very easy, but if by chance you have studied a little and know if it be only the different medical systems of treatment... there are the systems of different countries, the different systems of medicines, there are, you know, allopathy, homoeopathy, this one and that; so one tells you one thing, another tells you another. You know people who have told you, "Don't do this, do that", others who say, "Above all don't do this, do that", and so on, and so you find yourself facing the problem and ask yourself, "Well, with all that, what do I know myself, what am I going to decide? I know nothing."

There is only one thing which knows in you, that's your psychic; *it* makes no mistake, it will immediately, instantaneously tell you, if you obey it without a word and without your ideas and arguments, it will make you do the right thing. But all the rest... you are lost. And for everything: what are you going to study, what are you not going to study, what work are you going to do, what path are you going to take? But then there are all the possibilities which come in, all that you have either studied or met in life, all the suggestions you have received from all sides, which are there, like that, dancing around you. And with what will you decide? I am speaking of people who are absolutely sincere and have no preconceived ideas, prejudices, established rules which they follow in a mechanical routine, without endeavouring to know the truth at all, and for whom their mental construction is the truth. Then it is so simple, one goes straight on his path, bumps his nose against the wall but doesn't notice it until the nose is smashed. But otherwise it is terribly difficult.

This was what Sri Aurobindo meant when he said that one lived constantly in ignorance and that unless the mind of ignorance is replaced by mind of light one could not follow the true path, and that this was the indispensable preparation before any integral transformation could take place.

THE MOTHER

The Psychic Being — Centre for Self-Unification

The work of unifying the being consists of:

(1) becoming aware of one's psychic being.

(2) Putting before the psychic being, as one becomes aware of them, all one's movements, impulses, thoughts and acts of will, so that the psychic being may accept or reject each of these movements, impulses, thoughts or acts of will. Those that are accepted will be kept and carried out; those that are rejected will be driven out of the consciousness so that they may never come back again.

THE MOTHER

If we truly want to progress and acquire the capacity of knowing the truth of our being, that is to say, what we are truly created for, what we can call our mission upon earth, then we must, in a very regular and constant manner, reject from us or eliminate in us whatever contradicts the truth of our existence, whatever is opposed to it. In this way, little by little, all the parts, all the elements of our being can be organised into a homogeneous whole around our psychic centre. This work of unification requires much time to be brought to some degree of perfection. Therefore, in order to accomplish it, we must arm ourselves with patience and endurance, with a determination to prolong our life as long as necessary for the success of our endeavour.

As you pursue this labour of purification and unification, you must at the same time take great care to perfect the external and instrumental part of your being. When the higher truth manifests, it must find in you a mind that is supple and rich enough to be able to give the idea that seeks to express itself a form of thought which preserves its force and clarity. This thought, again, when it seeks to clothe itself in words, must find in you a sufficient power of expression so that the words reveal the thought and do not deform it. And the formula in which you embody the truth should be manifested in all your feelings, all your acts of will, all your actions, in all the movements of your being. Finally, these movements themselves should, by constant effort, attain their highest perfection.

All this can be realised by means of a fourfold discipline, the general outline of which is given here. The four aspects of the discipline do not exclude each other, and can be followed at the same time; indeed, this is preferable. The starting-point is what can be called the psychic discipline. We give the name "psychic" to the psychological centre of our being, the seat within us of the highest truth of our existence, that which can know this truth and set it in movement. It is therefore of capital importance to become conscious of its presence in us, to concentrate on this presence until it becomes a living fact for us and we can identify ourselves with it.

In various times and places many methods have been prescribed for attaining this perception and ultimately achieving this identification. Some methods are psychological, some religious, some even mechanical. In reality, everyone has to find the one which suits him best, and if one has an ardent and steadfast aspiration, a persistent and dynamic will, one is sure to meet, in one way or another — outwardly through reading and study, inwardly through concentration, meditation, revelation and experience — the help one needs to reach the goal. Only one thing is absolutely indispensable: the will to discover and to realise. This discovery and realisation should be the primary preoccupation of our being, the pearl of great price which we must acquire at any cost. Whatever you do, whatever your occupations and activities, the will to find the truth of your being and to unite with it must be always living and present behind all that you do, all that you feel, all that you think.

THE MOTHER

You say that it is necessary to establish "homogeneity in our being"?

Don't you know what a homogeneous thing is, made up of all similar parts? That means the whole being must be under the same influence, same consciousness, same tendency, same will. We are formed of all kinds of different pieces. They become active one after another. According to the part that is active, one is quite another person, becomes almost another personality. For instance, one had an aspiration at first, felt that everything existed only for the Divine, then something happens, somebody comes along, one has to do something, and everything disappears. One tries to recall the experience, not even the memory of the experience remains. One is completely under another influence, one wonders how this could have happened. There are examples of double, triple, quadruple personalities, altogether unconscious of themselves.... But it is not about this I am speaking; I am speaking about something which has happened to all of you: you have had an experience, and for some time you have felt, understood that this experience was the only thing that was important, that had an absolute value — half an hour later you try to recall it, it is like a smoke that vanishes. The experience has disappeared. And yet half an hour ago it was there and so powerful.... It is because one is made of all kinds of different things. The body is like a bag with pebbles and pearls all mixed up, and it is only the bag which keeps all that together. This is not a homogeneous, uniform consciousness but a heterogeneous one.

You can be a different person at different moments in your life. I know people who took decisions, had a strong will, knew what they wanted and prepared to do it. Then there is a little reversal in the being; another part came up and spoilt all the work in ten minutes. What had been accomplished in two months was all undone. When the first part comes back it is in dismay, it says: "What!..." Then the whole work has to be started again, slowly. Hence it is evident that it is very important to become aware of the psychic being; one must have a kind of signpost or a mirror in which all things are reflected and show themselves as they truly are. And then, according to what they are, one puts them in one place or another; one begins to explain, to organise. That takes time. The same part comes back three or four times and every part that comes up says: "Put me in the first place; what the others do is not important, not at all important, it is I who will decide, for I am the most important." I am sure that if you look at yourself, you will see that there's not one among you who has not had the experience. You want to become conscious, to have goodwill, you have understood,

Role, Function and Action of the Psychic

your aspiration is shining — all is brilliant, illuminated; but all of a sudden something happens, a useless conversation, some unfortunate reading, and that upsets everything. Then one thinks that it was an illusion one lived in, that all things were seen from a certain angle.

This is life. One stumbles and falls at the first occasion. One tells oneself: "Oh! One can't always be so serious", and when the other part returns, once again, one repents bitterly: "I was a fool, I have wasted my time, now I must begin again...." At times there is one part that's ill-humoured, in revolt, full of worries, and another which is progressive, full of surrender. All that, one after the other.

There is but one remedy: that signpost must always be there, a mirror well placed in one's feelings, impulses, all one's sensations. One sees them in this mirror. There are some which are not very beautiful or pleasant to look at; there are others which are beautiful, pleasant, and must be kept. This one does a hundred times a day if necessary. And it is very interesting. One draws a kind of big circle around the psychic mirror and arranges all the elements around it. If there is something that is not all right, it casts a sort of grey shadow upon the mirror: this element must be shifted, organised. It must be spoken to, made to understand, one must come out of that darkness. If you do that, you never get bored. When people are not kind, when one has a cold in the head, when one doesn't know one's lessons, and so on, one begins to look into this mirror. It is very interesting, one sees the canker. "I thought I was sincere!" — not at all.

Not a thing happens in life which is not interesting. This mirror is very, very well made. Do that for two years, three, four years, at times one must do it for twenty years. Then at the end of a few years, look back, turn your gaze upon what you were three years ago: "How I have changed!... Was I like that?..." It is very entertaining. "I could speak like that? I could talk like that, think like that?... But I was indeed stupid! How I have changed!" Isn't it very interesting, isn't it?

THE MOTHER

Section III

GROWTH AND DEVELOPMENT OF THE PSYCHIC

A Person persistent through the lapse of worlds,
Although the same for ever in many shapes
By the outward mind and unrecognisable,
Assuming names unknown in unknown climes
Imprints through Time upon the earth's worn page
A growing figure of its secret self,
And learns by experience what the spirit knew,
Till it can see its truth alive and God.

Sri Aurobindo
Savitri, Book II, Canto XIV

Evolution and the Psychic

"This terrestrial evolutionary working of Nature from Matter to Mind and beyond it has a double process: there is an outward visible process of physical evolution with birth as its machinery, — for each evolved form of body housing its own evolved power of consciousness is maintained and kept in continuity by heredity; there is, at the same time, an invisible process of soul evolution with rebirth into ascending grades of form and consciousness as its machinery. The first by itself would mean only a cosmic evolution; for the individual would be a quickly perishing instrument, and the race, a more abiding collective formulation, would be the real step in the progressive manifestation of the cosmic Inhabitant, the universal Spirit: rebirth is an indispensable condition for any long duration and evolution of the individual being in the earth-existence. Each grade of cosmic manifestation, each type of form that can house the indwelling Spirit, is turned by rebirth into a means for the individual soul, the psychic entity, to manifest more and more of its concealed consciousness; each life becomes a step in a victory over Matter by a greater progression of consciousness in it which shall make eventually Matter itself a means for the full manifestation of the Spirit."

Sri Aurobindo, The Life Divine

It is difficult to understand, Sweet Mother.

Ah!...
 If you take terrestrial history, all the forms of life have

appeared one after another in a general plan, a general programme, with the addition, always, of a new perfection and a greater consciousness. Take just animal forms — for that is easier to understand, they are the last before man — each animal that appeared had an additional perfection in its general nature — I don't mean in all the details — a greater perfection than the preceding ones, and the crowning point of the ascending march was the human form which, for the moment, from the point of view of consciousness, is the form most capable of manifesting consciousness; that is, the human form at its height, at the height of its possibilities, is capable of more consciousness than all preceding animal forms.

This is *one* of Nature's ways of evolution.

Sri Aurobindo told us last week that this Nature was following an ascending progression in order to manifest more and more the divine consciousness contained in all forms. So, with each new form that it produces, Nature makes a form capable of expressing more completely the spirit which this form contains. But if it were like this, a form comes, develops, reaches its highest point and is followed by another form; the others do not disappear, but the individual does not progress. The individual dog or monkey, for instance, belongs to a species which has its own peculiar characteristics; when the monkey or the man arrives at the height of its possibilities, that is, when a human individual becomes the best type of humanity, it will be finished; the individual will not be able to progress any farther. He belongs to the human species, he will continue to belong to it. So, from the point of view of terrestrial history there is a progress, for each spe-

Growth and Development of the Psychic

cies represents a progress compared with the preceding species; but from the point of view of the individual, there is no progress: he is born, he follows his development, dies and disappears. Therefore, to ensure the progress of the individual, it was necessary to find another means; this one was not adequate. But within the individual, contained in each form, there is an organisation of consciousness which is closer to and more directly under the influence of the inner divine Presence, and the form which is under this influence — this kind of inner concentration of energy — has a life independent of the physical form — this is what we generally call the "soul" or the "psychic being" — and since it is organised around the divine centre it partakes of the divine nature which is immortal, eternal. The outer body falls away, and this remains throughout every experience that it has in each life, and there is a progress from life to life, and it is the progress of the *same* individual. And this movement complements the other, in the sense that instead of a species which progresses relative to other species, it is an individual who passes through all the stages of progress of these species and can continue to progress even when the species have reached the limit of their possibilities and... stay there or disappear — it depends on the case — but they cannot go any farther, whereas the individual, having a life independent of the purely material form, can pass from one form to another and continue his progress *indefinitely*. That makes a double movement which completes itself. And that is why each individual has the possibility of reaching the utmost realisation, independent of the form to which he momentarily belongs.

THE MOTHER

In the previous stages of the evolution Nature's first care and effort had to be directed towards a change in the physical organisation, for only so could there be a change of consciousness; this was a necessity imposed by the insufficiency of the force of consciousness already in formation to effect a change in the body. But in man a reversal is possible, indeed inevitable; for it is through his consciousness, through its transmutation and no longer through a new bodily organism as a first instrumentation that the evolution can and must be effected. In the inner reality of things a change of consciousness was always the major fact, the evolution has always had a spiritual significance and the physical change was only instrumental; but this relation was concealed by the first abnormal balance of the two factors, the body of the external Inconscience outweighing and obscuring in importance the spiritual element, the conscious being. But once the balance has been righted, it is no longer the change of body that must precede the change of consciousness; the consciousness itself by its mutation will necessitate and operate whatever mutation is needed for the body. It has to be noted that the human mind has already shown a capacity to aid Nature in the evolution of new types of plant and animal; it has created new forms of its environment, developed by knowledge and discipline considerable changes in its own mentality. It is not an impossibility that man should aid Nature consciously also in his own spiritual and physical evolution and transformation. The urge to it is already there and partly effective, though still incompletely understood and accepted by the surface mentality; but one day it may understand, go deeper within itself and discover the means,

Growth and Development of the Psychic

the secret energy, the intended operation of the Consciousness-Force within which is the hidden reality of what we call Nature.

All these are conclusions that can be arrived at even from the observation of the outward phenomena of Nature's progression, her surface evolution of being and of consciousness in the physical birth and the body. But there is the other, the invisible factor; there is rebirth, the progress of the soul by ascent from grade to grade of the evolving existence, and in the grades to higher and higher types of bodily and mental instrumentation. In this progression the psychic entity is still veiled, even in man the conscious mental being, by its instruments, by mind and life and body; it is unable to manifest fully, held back from coming to the front where it can stand out as the master of its nature, obliged to submit to a certain determination by the instruments, to a domination of Purusha by Prakriti. But in man the psychic part of the personality is able to develop with a much greater rapidity than in the inferior creation, and a time can arrive when the soul-entity is close to the point at which it will emerge from behind the veil into the open and become the master of its instrumentation in Nature. But this will mean that the secret indwelling spirit, the Daemon, the Godhead within is on the point of emergence; and, when it emerges, it can hardly be doubted that its demand will be, as indeed it already is in the Mind itself when it undergoes the inner psychic influence, for a diviner, a more spiritual existence. In the nature of the earth-life where the Mind is an instrument of the Ignorance, this can only be effected by a change of consciousness, a transition from a foundation in Ignorance to a foundation in Knowledge, from the mental to a supramental consciousness, a supramental instrumentation of Nature.

SRI AUROBINDO

With regard to the evolution upwards, it is more correct to speak of the psychic presence than the psychic being. For it is the psychic presence which little by little becomes the psychic being. In each evolving form there is this presence, but it is not individualised. It is something which is capable of growth and follows the movement of the evolution. It is not a descent of the involution from above. It is formed progressively round the spark of Divine Consciousness which is meant to be the centre of a growing being which becomes the psychic being when it is at last individualised. It is this spark that is permanent and gathers round itself all sorts of elements for the formation of that individuality; the true psychic being is formed only when the psychic personality is fully grown, fully built up, round the eternal divine spark; it attains its culmination, its total fulfilment if and when it unites with a being or personality from above.

Below the human level there is, ordinarily, hardly any individual formation — there is only this presence, more or less....

Of course one cannot say that every man has got a psychic being, just as one cannot refuse to grant it to every animal. Many animals that have lived near man have some beginnings of it, while so often one comes across people who do not seem to be anything else than brutes.... But on the whole, the psychic in the true sense starts at the human stage: that is also why the Catholic religion declares that only man has a soul. In man alone there is the possibility of the psychic being growing to its full stature even so far as to be able in the end to join and unite with a descending being, a godhead from above.

THE MOTHER

Process of Psychic Growth and Development

It is the soul in us which turns always towards Truth, Good and Beauty, because it is by these things that it itself grows in stature; the rest, their opposites, are a necessary part of experience, but have to be outgrown in the spiritual increase of the being. The fundamental psychic entity in us has the delight of life and all experience as part of the progressive manifestation of the spirit, but the very principle of its delight of life is to gather out of all contacts and happenings their secret divine sense and essence, a divine use and purpose so that by experience our mind and life may grow out of the Inconscience towards a supreme consciousness, out of the divisions of the Ignorance towards an integralising consciousness and knowledge. It is there for that and it pursues from life to life its ever-increasing upward tendency and insistence; the growth of the soul is a growth out of darkness into light, out of falsehood into truth, out of suffering into its own supreme and universal Ananda.

SRI AUROBINDO

Let us take a divine spark which, through attraction, through affinity and selection, gathers around it a beginning of psychic consciousness (this work is already very perceptible in animals — don't think you are exceptional beings, that you alone have a psychic being and the rest of creation hasn't. It begins in the mineral, it is a little more developed in the plant, and in the animal there is a first glimmer of the psychic presence). Then there comes a moment when this psychic being is sufficiently developed to have an independent consciousness and a personal will. And then after innumerable lives more or less individualised, it becomes conscious of itself, of its movements and of the environment it has chosen for its growth. Arriving at a certain state of perception, it decides — generally at the last minute of the life it has just finished upon earth — the conditions in which its next life will be passed. Here I must tell you a very important thing: the psychic being can progress and form itself only in the physical life and upon earth. As soon as it leaves a body, it enters into a rest which lasts for a more or less long time according to its own choice and its degree of development — a rest for assimilation, for a passive progress so to say, a rest for passive growth which will allow this same psychic being to pass on to new experiences and make a more active progress. But after having finished one life (which usually ends only when it has done what it wanted to do), it will have chosen the environment where it will be born, the approximate place where it will be born, the conditions and the kind of life in which it will be born, and a very precise programme of the experiences through which it will have to pass to be able to make the progress it wants to make.

I am going to give you quite a concrete example. Let us take a psychic being that has decided, for some reason or other, to enter the body of a being destined to become king,

Growth and Development of the Psychic 83

because there is a whole series of experiences it can have only under those conditions. After having passed through these experiences of a king, it finds that there is a whole domain in which it cannot make a progress due to these very conditions of life where it is. So when it has finished its term upon earth and decides to go away, it decides that in its next life it will take birth in an ordinary environment and in ordinary conditions, neither high nor low, but such that the body which it will take up will be free to do what it likes. For I do not tell you anything new when I say that the life of a king is the life of a slave; a king is obliged to submit to a whole protocol and to all kinds of ceremonies to keep his prestige (it is perhaps very pleasant for vain people, but for a psychic being it is not pleasant, for this deprives it of the possibility of a large number of experiences). So having taken this decision, it carries in itself all the memories which a royal life can give it and it takes rest for the period it considers necessary (here, I must say that I am speaking of a psychic being exclusively occupied with itself, not one consecrated to a work, because in that case it is the work which decides the future lives and their conditions; I am speaking of a psychic being at work completing its development). Hence it decides that at a certain moment it will take a body. Having already had a number of experiences, it knows that in a certain country, a certain part of the consciousness has developed; in another, another part, and so on; so it chooses the place which offers it easy possibilities of development: the country, the conditions of living, the approximate nature of the parents, and also the condition of the body itself, its physical structure and the qualities it needs for its experiences. It takes rest, then at the required moment, wakes up and projects its consciousness upon earth centralising it in the chosen domain and the chosen conditions — or almost so; there is a small margin you know, for in the psychic consciousness one is too far away from the material physical consciousness to be able to see with a clear vision; it is an approximation. It does not make a mistake about the country or the environment and it sees quite clearly the inner vibrations of the people chosen, but there may happen to be a slight indecision. But if, just at this moment, there is a couple upon earth or rather a woman who has a psychic aspiration herself and, for some reason or other, without knowing why or how, would like to have an exceptional child, answering certain exceptional conditions; if at this moment there is this aspiration upon earth, it creates a vibration, a psychic light which the psychic being sees immediately and, without hesitation it rushes towards it. Then, from that moment (which is the moment of conception), it watches over the formation of the child, so that this formation may be as favourable as possible to the plan it has; consequently its influence is there over the child even before it appears in the physical world.

If all goes well, if there is no accident (accidents can always happen), if all goes well at the moment the child is about to be born, the psychic force (perhaps not in its totality, but a part of the psychic consciousness) rushes into the being and from its very first cry gives it a push towards the experiences it wants the child to acquire. The result is that even if the parents are not conscious, even if the child in its external consciousness is not quite conscious (a little child does not have the necessary brain for that, it forms slowly,

Growth and Development of the Psychic

little by little), in spite of that, it will be possible for the psychic influence to direct all the events, all the circumstances of the life of this child till the moment it becomes capable of coming into conscious contact with its psychic being (physically it is generally between the age of four and seven, sometimes sooner, sometimes almost immediately, but in such a case we deal with children who are not "children", who have "supernatural" qualities, as they say — they are not "supernatural", but simply the expression of the presence of the psychic being). But there are people who have not had the chance or rather the good fortune, if one may call it that, of meeting someone, physically, who could instruct them. And yet they have the feeling that every step of their existence, every circumstance of their life is arranged by someone conscious, so that they may make the maximum progress. When they need a certain circumstance, it comes; when they need to meet certain people, they come; when they need to read certain books, they find them within their reach. Everything is arranged like that, as if someone was watching over them so that their life may have the maximum possibilities of development. These people may very well say: "But what is a psychic being?", for no one has ever used these words in speaking to them or they have not found anybody who could explain to them all that; but for them often just one meeting is sufficient, just one look, in order to wake up; one word suffices to make them remember: "But I knew all that!"

This is exactly what happens to a psychic being which has reached the last stage of its development. After that, it will no longer be bound by the necessity of coming upon earth, it will have completed its development and will be able to choose freely either to consecrate itself to the divine Work or go elsewhere, that is, in the higher worlds. But generally, having come to this stage, it remembers all that has happened to it and understands the great necessity of coming to the help of those who are yet struggling in the midst of difficulties. These psychic beings give their whole existence to the divine Work — this is not absolute, inevitable, they choose freely, but ninety times out of a hundred this is what they do.

THE MOTHER

Each time that the soul takes birth in a new body it comes with the intention of having a new experience which will help it to develop and to perfect its personality. This is how the psychic being is formed from life to life and becomes a completely conscious and independent personality which, once it has arrived at the summit of its development, is free to choose not only the time of its incarnation, but the place, the purpose and the work to be accomplished.

Its descent into the physical body is necessarily a descent into darkness, ignorance, unconsciousness; and for a very long time it must labour simply to bring a little consciousness into the material substance of the body, before it can make use of it for the experience it has come for. So, if we cultivate the body by a clear-sighted and rational method, at the same time we are helping the growth of the soul, its progress and enlightenment.

THE MOTHER

Mother, since in each new life the mind and vital as well as the body are new, how can the experiences of past lives be

Growth and Development of the Psychic 87

useful for them? Do we have to go through all the experiences once again?

That depends on people!

It is not the mind and vital which develop and progress from life to life — except in altogether exceptional cases and at a very advanced stage of evolution — it is the psychic. So, this is what happens: the psychic has alternate periods of activity and rest; it has a life of progress resulting from experiences of the physical life, of active life in a physical body, with all the experiences of the body, the vital and the mind; then, normally, the psychic goes into a kind of rest for assimilation where the result of the progress accomplished during its active existence is worked out, and when this assimilation is finished, when it has absorbed the progress it had prepared in its active life on earth, it comes down again in a new body bringing with it the result of all its progress and, at an advanced stage, it even chooses the environment and the kind of body and the kind of life in which it will live to complete its experience concerning one point or another. In some very advanced cases the psychic can, before leaving the body, decide what kind of life it will have in its next incarnation. When it has become an almost completely formed and already very conscious being, it presides over the formation of the new body, and usually through an inner influence it chooses the elements and the substance which will form its body in such a way that the body is adapted to the needs of its new experience. But this is at a rather advanced stage. And later, when it is fully formed and returns to earth with the idea of service, of collective help and participation in the divine Work, then it is able to bring to the body in formation certain elements of the mind and vital from previous lives which, having been organised and impregnated with psychic forces in previous lives, could be preserved and, consequently, can participate in the general progress. But this is at a very, very advanced stage.

When the psychic is fully developed and very conscious, when it becomes a conscious instrument of the divine Will, it organises the vital and the mind in such a way that they too participate in the general harmony and can be preserved.

A high degree of development allows at least some parts of the mental and vital beings to be preserved in spite of the dissolution of the body. If, for instance, some parts — mental or vital — of the human activity have been particularly developed, these elements of the mind and vital are maintained even "in their form" — in the form of the activity which has been fully organised — as, for example, in highly intellectual people who have particularly developed their brains, the mental part of their being keeps this structure and is preserved in the form of an organised brain which has its own life and can be kept unchanged until a future life so as to participate in it with all its gains.

In artists, as for instance in certain musicians who have used their hands in a particularly conscious way, the vital and mental substance is preserved in the form of hands, and these hands remain fully conscious, they can even use the body of living people if there is a special affinity — and so on.

Otherwise, in ordinary people in whom the psychic form is not fully developed and organised, when the psychic leaves

Growth and Development of the Psychic

the body, the mental and vital forms may persist for a certain time if the death has been particularly peaceful and concentrated, but if a man dies suddenly and in a state of passion, with numerous attachments, well, the different parts of the being are dispersed and live for a shorter or longer time their own life in their own domain, then disappear.

The centre of organisation and transformation is always the presence of the psychic in the body. Therefore, it is a very big mistake to believe that the progress continues or even, as some believe, that it is more complete and rapid in the periods of transition between two physical lives; in general, there is no progress at all, for the psychic enters into a state of rest and the other parts, after a more or less ephemeral life in their own domain, are dissolved.

Earthly life is the place for progress. It is here, on earth, that progress is possible, during the period of earthly existence. And it is the psychic which carries the progress over from one life to another, by organising its own evolution and development itself.

THE MOTHER

If it is not the mind, vital or physical which take birth again but only the psychic being, then the vital or mental progress made before is of no value in another life?

It happens only to the extent the progress of these parts has brought them close to the psychic, that is, to the extent the progress lies in putting all the parts of the being successively under the psychic influence. For all that is under the psychic influence and identified with the psychic continues, and it is that alone which continues. But if the psychic is made the centre of one's life and consciousness, and if the whole being is organised around it, the whole being passes under the psychic influence, becomes united with it, and can continue — if it is necessary for it to continue. Indeed, if the physical body could be given the same movement — the same movements of progress and the same capacity to ascend that the psychic being has — well, it wouldn't be necessary for it to decompose. But that indeed is the difficulty.

And only that which is in contact with the psychic lasts, and only what can last can remember, for the rest disappears, is again dissolved into small pieces and utilised elsewhere — as the body is dissolved again to dust and used elsewhere. It goes back to the earth, plants use the soil, men eat the plants. It is in this way that it goes on. And then it returns to the earth and begins again. That's the way Nature progresses. In order to progress she makes a heap of forms, then, when that seems no longer important or necessary to her, she demolishes them, takes up all the elements again, chemical or other, and reconstitutes something else, and so it goes on changing all the time, coming and going. And she finds that very good, for she sees very far, her work extends over centuries, and a small human life is nothing, just a breath in eternity. So she takes up, shapes; she takes a certain time, it's fun for her, she finds it very good; and then, when it is no longer so good, she demolishes it — she takes up, mixes everything, begins another form, makes something else. And so perhaps with this process which is evidently very slow, finally the whole of matter progresses. It is possible — always in this way, intermingling, breaking up, remixing, breaking up again. Essentially, it is as though one made a heap of small objects and then destroyed them, remade something from the dust, remade other toys, and again broke them, and remade others out of that. Each time one adds something so that it mixes well. And then, one day, perhaps all that will produce something. In any case, she is in no hurry. And when we are in a hurry, she says: "Why are you in such a haste? It is sure to happen one day. You don't need to worry, it will surely come. Wait quietly." Then we tell her: "But it is not I who am waiting!" — "Ah! That's because you call 'I' that thing which comes and goes away. If you were to call consciousness — the one, eternal and divine consciousness — if you were to call that 'I', then you would see everything, you would be present at everything. Nobody prevents you from doing it! It is only because you identify yourself with this (*indicating the body*). You have only to stop identifying yourself with that."

THE MOTHER

Does the psychic being always progress?

There are in the psychic being two very different kinds of progress: one consisting in its formation, building and organisation. For the psychic starts by being only a kind of tiny divine spark inside the being and out of this spark will emerge progressively an independent conscious being having its own action and will. The psychic being at its origin is only a spark of the divine consciousness and it is through successive lives that it builds up a conscious individuality. It is a progress similar to that of a growing child. It is a thing in the making. For a long time, in most human beings the psychic is a being in the making. It is not a fully individualised, fully conscious being and master of itself and it needs all its rebirths, one after another, in order to build itself and become fully conscious.

But this sort of progress has an end. There comes a time when the being is fully developed, fully individualised, fully master of itself and its destiny. When this being or one of these psychic beings at that state, takes birth in a human being, that makes a very great difference: the human being, so to say, is born free. He is not tied to circumstances, to surroundings, to his origin and atavism, like ordinary people. He comes into the world with the purpose of doing something, with a work to carry out, a mission to fulfil. From this point of view his progress in growth has come to an end, that is, it is not indispensable for him to take birth again in a body. Till then rebirth is a necessity, for it is through rebirth that he grows; it is in the physical life and in a physical body that he gradually develops and becomes a fully conscious being. But once he is fully formed, he is free, in this sense that he can take birth or not, at will. So there, one kind of progress stops.

But if this fully formed being wants to become an instrument of work for the Divine, if instead of retiring to repose in a psychic bliss, in its own domain, he chooses to be a worker upon earth to help in the fulfilment of the Divine Work, then he has a fresh progress to make, a progress in the capacity for work, for organisation of his work and for expression of the Divine Will. So there is a time when the thing changes. So long as he remains in the world, so long as he chooses to work for the Divine, he will progress. Only if he with-

Growth and Development of the Psychic 93

draws into the psychic world and refuses to continue doing the Divine Work or renounces it, can he remain in a static condition outside all progress, because, as I have told you, only upon earth is there progress, only in the physical world; it is not acquired everywhere. In the psychic world there is a kind of blissful repose. One remains what one is, without any movement.

But for those who are not conscious of their psychic?

They are compelled to progress whether they want it or not.

The psychic being itself progresses in them and they are not conscious of it. But they themselves are compelled to progress. That is to say, they follow a curve. They follow an ascent in life. It is the same progress as that of the growing child; there comes a time when it is at the summit of its growth and then, unless it changes the plane of progress, unless the purely physical progress turns into a mental progress, a psychic progress, a spiritual progress, it goes down the curve and then there will be a decomposition and it will not exist any longer.

It is just because progress is not constant and perpetual in the physical world that there is a growth, an apogee, a decline and a decomposition. For anything that does not advance, falls back; all that does not progress, regresses.

So this is just what happens physically. The physical world has not learnt how to progress indefinitely; it arrives at a certain point, then it is either tired of progressing or is not capable of progressing in the present constitution, but in any case it stops progressing and after a time decomposes. Those who lead a purely physical life reach a kind of summit, then they slide down very quickly. But now, with the general collective human progress, there is behind the physical progress a vital progress and a mental progress, so that the mental progress can go on for a very long time, even after the physical progress has come to a stop, and through this mental progress one keeps up a kind of ascent long after the physical has ceased to progress.

And then there are those who do yoga, who become conscious of their psychic being, are united with it, participate in its life; these, indeed, progress till the last breath of their life. And they do not stop even after death, when they have left their body under the plea that the body cannot last any longer: they continue to progress.

It is the incapacity of the body to transform itself, to continue progressing that causes it to regress and in the end become more and more open to the inner disequilibrium until one day that becomes strong enough to bring about a total imbalance and it can no longer regain its balance and health.... It is only in the pure spiritual life — that which is outside all physical and terrestrial existence, including the mental — that there is no progress. You reach a static state and are outside all movements of progress. But at the same time you are outside the manifestation also. When you reach that state, you no longer belong to the manifestation, you go out of the manifested world. One must go out of the manifested world in order to go out of all progress, because the two are identical: manifestation means progress and progress means manifestation.

THE MOTHER

In what does a psychic being's progress consist?

Individualisation, the capacity to take up all experiences and organise them around the divine centre.

The aim of the psychic being is to form an individual being, individualised, "personalised" around the divine centre. Normally, all the experiences of the external life (unless one does yoga and becomes conscious) pass without organising the inner being, while the psychic being organises these experiences serially. It wants to realise a particular attitude towards the Divine. Hence it looks for all favourable experiences in order to have the complete series of opportunities, so to say, which will allow it to realise this attitude towards the Divine. Take someone, for example, who wants to have the experience of nobility — a nobility which makes it impossible for you to act like an ordinary person, which infuses into you a bravery, a courage which may almost be taken for rashness because the attitude, the experience demands that you face danger without showing the least fear. I was telling you a while ago that I would explain to you what one could acquire by entering into the body of a king. A king is an ordinary man, isn't he, like all others, he does not have a special consciousness, but through the necessities of his life, because he is a kind of symbol to his people, there are things he is obliged to do which he could never do if he were an ordinary man. I know this by experience, but I saw this also while looking at photographs which represented a king in actual circumstances: something had happened, which might have been an attempt on his life, but was averted. The photographs showed the king inspecting a regiment; all of a sudden someone had rushed forward, perhaps with a bad intention, perhaps not, for nothing had happened; in any case, the king had remained completely impassive, absolutely calm, the same smile on his lips, without moving the least from the place where he was; and he was quite within sight, an easy target for one who wanted to rush forward and hurt him. For all I know, this king was not a hero, but because he was a king, he could not take to flight! That would have been ignoble. So he remained calm, without stirring, without showing any outward fear. This is an example of what one can learn in the life of a king.

There is also a true story about Queen Elizabeth. She had come to the last days of her life and was extremely ill. But there was trouble in the country and, about questions of taxation, a group of people (merchants, I believe) had formed a delegation to present a petition to her in the name of a party of the people. She lay very ill in her room, so ill that she could hardly stand. But she got up and dressed to receive them. The lady who was attending upon her cried out, "But it is impossible, you will die of this!" The queen answered quietly, "We shall die afterwards".... This is an example from a whole series of experiences one can have in the life of a king, and it is this which justifies the choice of the psychic being when it takes up this kind of life.

It is memories of this kind which prove the authenticity of the experience; for what generally happens when people tell you about their past lives is this: in these lives there is always a progress, naturally; so they become more and more splendid people in more and more marvellous circumstances! It is wrong, things never happen like that. The psychic being

Growth and Development of the Psychic

follows a certain line of existence which develops certain qualities, certain powers, etc., but the psychic being always sees what it lacks and it can choose the opposite line in a future life, a negation, so to say, of this experience in order to have complementary experiences.

THE MOTHER

"The mind's door of entry to the conception of him [the Divine] must necessarily vary according to the past evolution and the present nature."

Sri Aurobindo, *The Synthesis of Yoga*

That is, the evolution in former lives and the present nature, that is, the nature of the present body, determine one's approach to the Divine.

We can take a very... an over-simple example. If one is born in any particular religion, quite naturally the first effort to approach the Divine will be within that religion; or else if in former lives one has passed through a certain number of experiences which determined the necessity of another kind of experiences, quite naturally one will follow the path which leads to those experiences.

You see, the life of the psychic being is made up of successive experiences in successive physical existences. So, it may be put a little childishly or romantically: you have a psychic which for some reason or other has incarnated so as to be able to have all the experiences which royalty gives — for instance, supreme power. After it has had its experience, has had what it wanted, it can, before leaving the body, decide that in the next life it will take birth in obscure conditions, because it needs to have experiences which can be had in a modest condition, and with the freedom one feels when he has no responsibilities, you see, responsibilities like those the heads of states have, for instance. So quite naturally, in its next life it will be born in certain conditions which fulfil its need. And it is in accordance with this experience that it will approach the Divine.

Then, in addition, it is the product of the union of two physical natures, you know, and sometimes of two vital natures. The result of this is more or less a kind of mixture of these natures; but it brings about a tendency, what is called a character. Well, this character will make it fit for a certain field, a certain category of experiences.

So with what has been determined, decided in former lives or in a former life, and then the environment in which it is born — that is, the conditions in which its present body has been formed — its approach to and search for the Divine will be in accordance with a definite line which is its own, and which, naturally, is not at all the same as that of its neighbour or any other being.

I said a while ago: each individual is a special manifestation in the universe, therefore his true path must be an absolutely unique path. There are similarities, there are resemblances, there are categories, families, churches, ideals also, that is, a certain collective way of approaching the Divine, which creates a kind of church, not materialised but in a more subtle world — there are all these things — but for the details of the path, the details of yoga, it will be different according to each individual, necessarily, and conditioned physically by his present bodily structure, and vitally, mentally and psychically, of course, by former lives.

THE MOTHER

How can one make one's psychic personality grow?

It is through all the experiences of life that the psychic personality forms, grows, develops and finally becomes a complete, conscious and free being.

This process of development goes on tirelessly through innumerable lives, and if one is not conscious of it, it is because one is not conscious of one's psychic being — for that is the indispensable starting-point. Through interiorisation and concentration one has to enter into conscious contact with one's psychic being. This psychic being always has an influence on the outer being, but that influence is almost always occult, neither seen nor perceived nor felt, save on truly exceptional occasions.

In order to strengthen the contact and aid, if possible, the development of the conscious psychic personality, one should, while concentrating, turn towards it, aspire to know it and feel it, open oneself to receive its influence, and take great care, each time that one receives an indication from it, to follow it very scrupulously and sincerely. To live in a great aspiration, to take care to become inwardly calm and remain so always as far as possible, to cultivate a perfect sincerity in all the activities of one's being — these are the essential conditions for the growth of the psychic being.

THE MOTHER

Section IV

THE PSYCHIC BEING AND SADHANA

Earth must transform herself and equal Heaven
Or Heaven descend into earth's mortal state.
But for such vast spiritual change to be,
Out of the mystic cavern in man's heart
The heavenly Psyche must put off her veil
And step into common nature's crowded rooms
And stand uncovered in that nature's front
And rule its thoughts and fill the body and life.

SRI AUROBINDO
Savitri, Book VII, Canto II

Three Steps of Self-Realisation and the Triple Transformation

In the spiritual knowledge of self there are three steps of its self-achievement which are at the same time three parts of the one knowledge. The first is the discovery of the soul, not the outer soul of thought and emotion and desire, but the secret psychic entity, the divine element within us. When that becomes dominant over the nature, when we are consciously the soul and when mind, life and body take their true place as its instruments, we are aware of a guide within that knows the truth, the good, the true delight and beauty of existence, controls heart and intellect by its luminous law and leads our life and being towards spiritual completeness. Even within the obscure workings of the Ignorance we have then a witness who discerns, a living light that illumines, a will that refuses to be misled and separates the mind's truth from its error, the heart's intimate response from its vibrations to a wrong call and wrong demand upon it, the life's true ardour and plenitude of movement from vital passion and the turbid falsehoods of our vital nature and its dark self-seekings. This is the first step of self-realisation, to enthrone the soul, the divine psychic individual in the place of the ego. The next step is to become aware of the eternal self in us unborn and one with the self of all beings. This self-realisation liberates and universalises; even if our action still proceeds in the dynamics of the Ignorance, it no longer binds or misleads because our inner being is seated in the light of self-knowledge. The third step is to know the Divine Being who is at once our supreme transcendent Self, the Cosmic Being, foundation of our universality, and the Divinity within of which our psychic being, the true evolving individual in our nature, is a portion, a spark, a flame growing into the eternal Fire from which it was lit and of which it is the witness ever living within us and the conscious instrument of its light and power and joy and beauty.

SRI AUROBINDO

There are a thousand ways of approaching and realising the Divine and each way has its own experiences which have their own truth and stand really on a basis one in essence but complex in aspects, common to all but not expressed in the same way by all. There is not much use in discussing these variations; the important thing is to follow one's own way well and thoroughly. In this yoga, one can realise the psychic being as a portion of the Divine seated in the heart with the Divine supporting it there — this psychic being takes charge of the sadhana and turns the whole being to the Truth, the Divine, with results in the mind, the vital and the physical consciousness which I need not go into here — that is the first transformation. We realise next the one Self, Brahman, Divine, first *above* the body, life, mind and not only within the heart supporting them — above and free and unattached as the static Self in all and dynamic too as the active Divine Being and Power, Ishwara-Shakti, containing the world and pervading it as well as transcending it, manifesting all cosmic aspects. But what is most important for us is that it manifests as a transcending Light, Knowledge, Power, Purity, Peace, Ananda of which we become aware and which descends into the being and progressively replaces the ordinary consciousness itself by its own movements — that is the second transformation.

We realise also the consciousness itself as moving upward, ascending through many planes, physical, vital, mental, overmental to the supramental and Ananda planes. This is nothing new; it is stated in the Taittiriya Upanishad that there are five Purushas, the physical, the vital, the mental, the Truth Purusha (supramental) and the Bliss Purusha; it says that one has to draw the physical self into the vital self, the vital into the mental, the mental into the Truth self, the Truth self into the Bliss self and so attain perfection. But in this yoga we become aware not only of this taking up but of a pouring down of the power of the higher Self, so that there comes in the possibility of a descent of the supramental Self and Nature to dominate and change our present nature and turn it from nature of Ignorance into nature of Truth-Knowledge (and through the supramental into nature of Ananda) — this is the third or supramental transformation. It does not always go in this order, for with many the spiritual descent begins first in an imperfect way before the psychic is in front and in charge, but the psychic development has to be attained before a perfect and unhampered spiritual descent can take place, and the last or supramental change is impossible so long as the two first have not become full and complete. That's the whole matter put as briefly as possible.

Sri Aurobindo

Becoming Conscious of the Psychic Being — Need for Sadhana

In the ordinary life there's not one person in a million who has a conscious contact with his psychic being, even momentarily. The psychic being may work from within, but so invisibly and unconsciously for the outer being that it is as though it did not exist. And in most cases, the immense majority, almost the totality of cases, it's as though it were asleep, not at all active, in a kind of torpor.

It is only with the sadhana and a very persistent effort that one succeeds in having a conscious contact with his psychic being. Naturally, it is possible that there are exceptional cases — but this is truly exceptional, and they are so few that they could be counted — where the psychic being is an entirely formed, liberated being, master of itself, which has chosen to return to earth in a human body in order to do its work. And in this case, even if the person doesn't do the sadhana consciously, it is possible that the psychic being is powerful enough to establish a more or less conscious relation. But these cases are, so to say, unique and are exceptions which confirm the rule.

In almost, almost all cases, a very very sustained effort is needed to become aware of one's psychic being. Usually it is considered that if one can do it in thirty years one is very lucky — thirty years of sustained effort, I say. It may happen that it's quicker. But this is so rare that immediately one says, "This is not an ordinary human being." That's the case of people who have been considered more or less divine beings and who were great yogis, great initiates.

THE MOTHER

You wrote to me that it is not easy to come in contact with the psychic being. Why do You consider it difficult? How should I begin?

The Psychic Being and Sadhana

I said "not easy" because the contact is not spontaneous — it is voluntary. The psychic being always has an influence on the thoughts and actions, but one is rarely conscious of it. To become conscious of the psychic being, one must want to do so, make one's mind as silent as possible, and enter deep into the heart of one's being, beyond sensations and thoughts. One must form the habit of silent concentration and descent into the depths of one's being.

The discovery of the psychic being is a definite and very concrete fact, as all who have had the experience know.

THE MOTHER

The Psychic Being and Conversion

The psychic being is always there, but is not felt because it is covered up by the mind and vital; when it is no longer covered up, it is then said to be awake. When it is awake, it begins to take hold of the rest of the being, to influence it and change it so that all may become the true expression of the inner soul. It is this change that is called the inner conversion. There can be no conversion without the awakening of the psychic being.

SRI AUROBINDO

The conversion which keeps the consciousness turned towards the light and makes the right attitude spontaneous and natural and abiding and rejection also spontaneous is the psychic conversion. That is to say, man usually lives in his vital and the body is its instrument and the mind its counsellor and minister (except for the few mental men who live mostly for the things of the mind, but even they are in subjection to the vital in their ordinary movements). The spiritual conversion begins when the soul begins to insist on a deeper life and is complete when the psychic being becomes the basis or the leader of the consciousness and mind and vital and body are led by it and obey it.

SRI AUROBINDO

Consecration is a process by which one trains the consciousness to give itself to the Divine. But conversion is a spontaneous movement of the consciousness, a turning of it away from external things towards the Divine. It comes as well as is the result of a touch from within and above. Self-consecration may help one to open to the touch or the touch may come of itself. But conversion may also come as the culmination of a long process of aspiration and Tapasya. There is no fixed rule in these things.

If the psychic being comes to the front, then conversion becomes easy or may come instantaneously or the conversion may bring the psychic being to the front. Here, again, there is no rule.

It may be either way, there is a touch and the realisation also and the psychic takes its proper place as the result or the psychic may come to the front and prepare the nature for the realisation.

Transformation is something progressive, but certainly there must be realisation before the aim of the transformation is possible.

SRI AUROBINDO

Psychic Change — First Necessity

The soul, the psychic being is in direct touch with the divine Truth, but it is hidden in man by the mind, the vital being and the physical nature. One may practise yoga and get illuminations in the mind and the reason; one may conquer power and luxuriate in all kinds of experiences in the vital; one may establish even surprising physical Siddhis; but if the true soul-power behind does not manifest, if the psychic nature does not come into the front, nothing genuine has been done. In this yoga the psychic being is that which opens the rest of the nature to the true supramental light and finally to the supreme Ananda. Mind can open by itself to its own higher reaches; it can still itself and widen into the Impersonal; it may too spiritualise itself in some kind of static liberation or Nirvana; but the supramental cannot find a sufficient base in a spiritualised mind alone. If the inmost soul is awakened, if there is a new birth out of the mere mental, vital and physical into the psychic consciousness, then this yoga can be done; otherwise (by the sole power of the mind or any other part) it is impossible.

Sri Aurobindo

It is certainly better if the psychic is conscious and active before there is the removing of the veil or screen between the individual and the universal consciousness which comes when the inner being is brought forward in all its wideness. For then there is much less danger of the difficulties of what I have called the Intermediate Zone.

Sri Aurobindo

Everything is dangerous in the sadhana or can be, except the psychic change.

SRI AUROBINDO

Purification and consecration are two great necessities of sadhana. Those who have experiences before purification run a great risk: it is much better to have the heart pure first, for then the way becomes safe. That is why I advocate the psychic change of the nature first — for that means the purification of the heart: the turning of it wholly to the Divine, the subjection of the mind and the vital to the control of the inner being, the soul. Always, when the soul is in front, one gets the right guidance from within as to what is to be done, what avoided, what is the wrong thing or the true thing in thought, feeling, action. But this inner intimation emerges in proportion as the consciousness grows more and more pure.

SRI AUROBINDO

I have read your account of your sadhana. There is nothing to say, I think, — for it is all right — except that the most important thing for you is to develop the psychic fire in the heart and the aspiration for the psychic being to come forward as the leader of the sadhana. When the psychic does so, it will show you the "undetected ego-knots" of which you speak and loosen them or burn them in the psychic fire. This psychic development and the psychic change of mind, vital and physical consciousness is of the utmost importance because it makes safe and easy the descent of the higher consciousness and the spiritual transformation without which the supramental must always remain far distant. Powers etc. have their place, but a very minor one so long as this is not done.

SRI AUROBINDO

As for experiences, they are all right but the trouble is that they do not seem to change the nature, they only enrich the consciousness — even the realisation, on the mind level, of the Brahman seems to leave the nature almost where it was, except for a few. That is why we insist on the psychic transformation as the first necessity — for that does change the nature — and its chief instrument is bhakti, surrender, etc.

SRI AUROBINDO

Emergence of the Psychic — Bringing Forward the Psychic

The true central being is the soul, but this being stands back and in most human natures is only the secret witness or, one might say, a constitutional ruler who allows his ministers to rule for him, delegates to them his empire, silently assents to their decisions and only now and then puts in a word which they can at any moment override and act otherwise. But this is so long as the soul-personality put forward by the psychic entity is not yet sufficiently developed; when this is strong enough for the inner entity to impose itself through it, then the soul can come forward and control the nature. It is by the coming forward of this true monarch and his taking up of the reins of government that there can take place a real harmonisation of our being and our life.

A first condition of the soul's complete emergence is a direct contact in the surface being with the spiritual Reality.

Because it comes from that, the psychic element in us turns always towards whatever in phenomenal Nature seems to belong to a higher Reality and can be accepted as its sign and character. At first, it seeks this Reality through the good, the true, the beautiful, through all that is pure and fine and high and noble: but although this touch through outer signs and characters can modify and prepare the nature, it cannot entirely or most inwardly and profoundly change it. For such an inmost change the direct contact with the Reality itself is indispensable since nothing else can so deeply touch the foundations of our being and stir it or cast the nature by its stir into a ferment of transmutation. Mental representations, emotional and dynamic figures have their use and value; Truth, Good and Beauty are in themselves primary and potent figures of the Reality, and even in their forms as seen by the mind, as felt by the heart, as realised in the life can be lines of an assent: but it is in a spiritual substance and being of them and of itself that That which they represent has to come into our experience.

SRI AUROBINDO

The soul in itself contains all possible strength, but most of it is held behind the veil and it is what comes forward in the nature that makes the difference. In some people the psychic element is strong and in others weak; in some people the mind is the strongest part and governs, in others the vital is the strongest part and leads or drives. But by sadhana the psychic being can be more and more brought forward till it is dominant and governs the rest. If it were already governing, then the struggles and difficulties of the mind and vital would

The Psychic Being and Sadhana

not at all be severe; for each man in the light of the psychic would see and feel the truth and more and more follow it.

SRI AUROBINDO

What is meant by [the psychic's] coming to the front is simply this. The psychic ordinarily is deep within. Very few people are aware of their souls — when they speak of their soul, they usually mean the vital + mental being or else the (false) soul of desire. The psychic remains behind and acts only through the mind, vital and physical wherever it can. For this reason the psychic being except where it is very much developed has only a small and partial, concealed and mixed or diluted influence on the life of most men. By coming forward is meant that it comes from behind the veil, its presence is felt already in the waking daily consciousness, its influence fills, dominates, transforms the mind and vital and their movements, even the physical. One is aware of one's soul, feels the psychic to be one's true being, the mind and the rest begin to be only instruments of the inmost within us.

SRI AUROBINDO

It seems to me that you must know by this time about the psychic being — that it is behind the veil and its consciousness also; only a little comes out in the mind and vital and physical. When that consciousness is not concealed, when you are aware of your soul (the psychic being), when its feelings and consciousness are yours, then you have got the consciousness of the psychic being. The feelings and aspirations of the psychic being are all turned towards truth and right consciousness and the Divine; it is the only part that cannot be touched by the hostile forces and their suggestions.

SRI AUROBINDO

The psychic being emerges slowly in most men, even after taking up sadhana. There is so much in the mind and vital that has to change and readjust itself before the psychic can be entirely free. One has to wait till the necessary process has gone far enough before it can burst its agelong veil and come in front to control the nature. It is true that nothing can give so much inner happiness and joy — though peace can come by the mental and vital liberation or through the growth of a strong *samatā* in the being.

SRI AUROBINDO

How can one know that the psychic being is in front?

My child, when it happens, one understands. It is exactly so long as one doesn't understand that it means that it hasn't come. This is like people asking you, "How can I know whether I am in contact with the Divine?" That itself is enough to prove that they are not. For if they are they can no longer ask the question. It is something understood. For the psychic it is the same thing. When the psychic is in front one knows it, and there is no possibility of any doubt. Consequently one no longer asks the question.

THE MOTHER

The sense of release as if from jail always accompanies the emergence of the psychic being or the realisation of the self above. It is therefore spoken of as a liberation, *mukti*. It is a

The Psychic Being and Sadhana

release into peace, happiness, the soul's freedom not tied down by the thousand ties and cares of the outward ignorant existence.

SRI AUROBINDO

Once the psychic has come to the front, can it withdraw again?

Yes. Generally one has a series of experiences of identification, very intense at first, which later gradually diminish, and then one day you find that they have disappeared. Still you must not be disturbed, for it is quite a common phenomenon. But next time — the second time — the contact is more easily obtained. And then comes a moment, which is not very far off, when as soon as one concentrates and aspires, one gets a contact. One may not have the power of keeping it all the time, but can get it at will. Then, from that moment things become very easy. When one feels a difficulty or there is a problem to be solved, when one wants to make progress or there is just a depression to conquer or an obstacle to be overcome or else simply for the joy of identification (for it is an experience that gives a very concrete joy; at the moment of identification one truly feels a very, very great joy), then, at any moment whatever, one may pause, concentrate for a while and aspire, and quite naturally the contact is established and all problems which were to be solved are solved. Simply to concentrate — to sit down and concentrate — to aspire in this way, and the contact is made, so to say, instantaneously.

There comes a time, as I said, when this does not leave you, that is, it is in the depths of the consciousness and supports all that you do, and you never lose the contact. Then many things disappear. For instance, depression is one of these things, discontentment, revolt, fatigue, depression, all these difficulties. And if one makes it a habit to step back, as we say, in one's consciousness and see on the screen of one's psychic consciousness — see all the circumstances, all the events, all the ideas, all the knowledge, everything — at that moment one sees *that* and has an altogether sure guide for everything that one may do. But this, perforce, takes a very long time to come.

THE MOTHER

Aspiration, constant and sincere, and will to turn to the Divine alone are the best means to bring forward the psychic.

SRI AUROBINDO

If desire is rejected and no longer governs the thought, feeling or action and there is a steady aspiration of an entirely sincere self-giving, the psychic usually after a time opens of itself.

SRI AUROBINDO

These things, anger, jealousy, desire are the very stuff of the ordinary human vital consciousness. They could not be changed if there were not a deeper consciousness within which is of quite another character. There is within you a psychic being which is divine, directly a part of the Mother, pure of all these defects. It is covered and concealed by the ordinary consciousness and nature, but when it is unveiled and able to come forward and govern the being, then it changes the ordinary consciousness, throws all these undivine

The Psychic Being and Sadhana

things out and changes the outer nature altogether. That is why we want the sadhaks to concentrate, to open this concealed consciousness — it is by concentration of whatever kind and the experiences it brings that one opens and becomes aware within and the new consciousness and nature begin to grow and come out. Of course we want them also to use their will and reject the desires and wrong movements of the vital, for by doing that the emergence of the true consciousness becomes possible. But rejection alone cannot succeed; it is by rejection and by inner experience and growth that it is done.

SRI AUROBINDO

You have asked what is the discipline to be followed in order to convert the mental seeking into a living spiritual experience. The first necessity is the practice of concentration of your consciousness within yourself. The ordinary human mind has an activity on the surface which veils the real Self. But there is another, a hidden consciousness within behind the surface one in which we can become aware of the real Self and of a larger deeper truth of nature, can realise the Self and liberate and transform the nature. To quiet the surface mind and begin to live within is the object of this concentration. Of this true consciousness other than the superficial there are two main centres, one in the heart (not the physical heart, but the cardiac centre in the middle of the chest), one in the head. The concentration in the heart opens within and by following this inward opening and going deep one becomes aware of the soul or psychic being, the divine element in the individual. This being unveiled begins to come forward, to govern the nature, to turn it and all its movements towards the Truth, towards the Divine, and to call down into it all that is above. It brings the consciousness of the Presence, the dedication of the being to the Highest and invites the descent into our nature of a greater Force and Consciousness which is waiting above us. To concentrate in the heart centre with the offering of oneself to the Divine and the aspiration for this inward opening and for the Presence in the heart is the first way and, if it can be done, the natural beginning; for its result once obtained makes the spiritual path far more easy and safe than if one begins the other way.

That other way is the concentration in the head, in the mental centre. This, if it brings about the silence of the surface mind, opens up an inner, larger, deeper mind within which is more capable of receiving spiritual experience and spiritual knowledge. But once concentrated here one must open the silent mental consciousness upward to all that is above mind. After a time one feels the consciousness rising upward and in the end it rises beyond the lid which has so long kept it tied in the body and finds a centre above the head where it is liberated into the Infinite. There it begins to come into contact with the universal Self, the Divine Peace, Light, Power, Knowledge, Bliss, to enter into that and become that, to feel the descent of these things into the nature. To concentrate in the head with the aspiration for quietude in the mind and the realisation of the Self and Divine above is the second way of concentration. It is important, however, to remember that the concentration of the consciousness in the head is only a preparation for its rising to the centre above; otherwise, one may get shut up in one's own mind and its

The Psychic Being and Sadhana

experiences or at best attain only to a reflection of the Truth above instead of rising into the spiritual transcendence to live there. For some the mental concentration is easier, for some the concentration in the heart centre; some are capable of doing both alternately — but to begin with the heart centre, if one can do it, is the more desirable.

The other side of discipline is with regard to the activities of the nature, of the mind, of the life-self or vital, of the physical being. Here the principle is to accord the nature with the inner realisation so that one may not be divided into two discordant parts. There are here several disciplines or processes possible. One is to offer all the activities to the Divine and call for the inner guidance and the taking up of one's nature by a Higher Power. If there is the inward soul-opening, if the psychic being comes forward, then there is no great difficulty — there comes with it a psychic discrimination, a constant intimation, finally a governance which discloses and quietly and patiently removes all imperfections, brings the right mental and vital movements and reshapes the physical consciousness also. Another method is to stand back detached from the movements of the mind, life, physical being, to regard their activities as only a habitual formation of general Nature in the individual imposed on us by past workings, not as any part of our real being; in proportion as one succeeds in this, becomes detached, sees mind and its activities as not oneself, life and its activities as not oneself, the body and its activities as not oneself, one becomes aware of an inner Being within us — inner mental, inner vital, inner physical — silent, calm, unbound, unattached which reflects the true Self above and can be its direct representative; from this inner silent Being proceeds a rejection of all that is to be rejected, an acceptance only of what can be kept and transformed, an inmost Will to perfection or a call to the Divine Power to do at each step what is necessary for the change of the Nature. It can also open mind, life and body to the inmost psychic entity and its guiding influence or its direct guidance. In most cases these two methods emerge and work together and finally fuse into one. But one can begin with either, the one that one feels most natural and easy to follow.

Finally, in all difficulties where personal effort is hampered, the help of the Teacher can intervene and bring about what is needed for the realisation or for the immediate step that is necessary.

SRI AUROBINDO

One can concentrate in any of the three centres which is easiest to the sadhak or gives most result. The power of the concentration in the heart-centre is to open that centre and by the power of aspiration, love, bhakti, surrender remove the veil which covers and conceals the soul and bring forward the soul or psychic being to govern the mind, life and body and turn and open them all fully to the Divine, removing all that is opposed to that turning and opening.

This is what is called in this yoga the psychic transformation. The power of concentration above the head is to bring peace, silence, liberation from the body sense, the identification with mind and life and open the way for the lower (mental, vital, physical) consciousness to rise up to meet the higher consciousness above and for the powers of the higher (spiritual nature) consciousness to descend into mind, life and

The Psychic Being and Sadhana

body. This is what is called in this yoga the spiritual transformation. If one begins with this movement then the Power from above has in its descent to open all the centres (including the lowest centre) and to bring out the psychic being; for until that is done there is likely to be much difficulty and struggle of the lower consciousness obstructing, mixing with or even refusing the Divine Action from above. If the psychic being is once active this struggle and these difficulties can be greatly minimised.

The power of concentration in the eyebrows is to open the centre there, liberate the inner mind and vision and the inner or yogic consciousness and its experiences and powers. From here also one can open upwards and act also in the lower centres; but the danger of this process is that one may get shut up in one's mental spiritual formations and not come out of them into the free and integral spiritual experience and knowledge and integral change of the being and nature.

Sri Aurobindo

The realisation of the psychic being, its awakening and the bringing of it in front depend mainly on the extent to which one can develop a personal relation with the Divine, a relation of Bhakti, love, reliance, self-giving, rejection of the insistences of the separating and self-asserting mental, vital and physical ego.

Sri Aurobindo

The Sunlit Way of the Psychic

There are always two ways of doing the yoga — one by the action of a vigilant mind and vital seeing, observing, thinking and deciding what is or is not to be done. Of course it acts with the Divine force behind it, drawing or calling in that Force — for otherwise nothing much can be done. But still it is the personal effort that is prominent and assumes most of the burden.

The other way is that of the psychic being, the consciousness opening to the Divine, not only opening the psychic and bringing it forward, but opening the mind, the vital and the physical, receiving the Light, perceiving what is to be done, feeling and seeing it done by the Divine Force itself and helping constantly by its own vigilant and conscious assent to and call for the divine working.

Usually there cannot but be a mixture of these two ways until the consciousness is ready to be entirely open, entirely submitted to the Divine's origination of all its action. It is then that all responsibility disappears and there is no personal burden on the shoulders of the sadhak.

SRI AUROBINDO

When the psychic is in the front, the sadhana becomes natural and easy and it is only a question of time and natural development. When the mind or the vital or the physical consciousness is on the top, then the sadhana is a tapasya and a struggle.

SRI AUROBINDO

The Psychic Being and Sadhana

The yoga is very usually a series of ups and downs till you get to a certain height. But there is a quite different reason for that — not the vagaries of the soul. On the contrary, when the psychic being gets in front and becomes master, there comes in a fundamentally smooth action and although there are difficulties and undulations of movement, these are no longer of an abrupt or dramatic character.

SRI AUROBINDO

If the psychic is awake and in front, it becomes easy to remain conscious of the things that have to be changed in the external nature and it is comparatively easy to change them. But if the psychic gets veiled and retires in the background, the outer nature left to itself finds it difficult to remain conscious of its own wrong movements and even with great effort cannot succeed in getting rid of them. You can see yourself, as in the matter of the food, that with the psychic active and awake the right attitude comes naturally and whatever difficulty there was soon diminishes or even disappears.

SRI AUROBINDO

It is not the soul that suffers; the self is calm and equal to all things and the only sorrow of the psychic being is the sorrow of the resistance of Nature to the Divine Will or the resistance of things and people to the call of the True, the Good and the Beautiful. What is affected by suffering is the vital nature and the body. When the soul draws towards the Divine, there may be a resistance in the mind and the common form of that is denial and doubt — which may create mental and vital suffering. There may again be a resistance in the vital nature whose principal character is desire and the attachment to the objects of desire, and if in this field there is conflict between the soul and the vital nature, between the Divine Attraction and the pull of the Ignorance, then obviously there may be much suffering of the mind and vital parts. The physical consciousness also may offer a resistance which is usually that of a fundamental inertia, an obscurity in the very stuff of the physical, an incomprehension, an inability to respond to the higher consciousness, a habit of helplessly responding to the lower mechanically, even when it does not want to do so; both vital and physical suffering may be the consequence. There is, moreover, the resistance of the Universal Nature which does not want the being to escape from the Ignorance into the Light. This may take the form of a vehement insistence in the continuation of the old movements, waves of them thrown on the mind and vital and body so that old ideas, impulses, desires, feelings, responses continue even after they are thrown out and rejected, and can return like an invading army from outside, until the whole nature, given to the Divine, refuses to admit them. This is the subjective form of the universal resistance, but it may also take an objective form, — opposition, calumny, attacks, persecution, misfortunes of many kinds, adverse conditions and circumstances, pain, illness, assaults from men or forces. There too the possibility of suffering is evident. There are two ways to meet all that — first that of the Self, calm, equality, a spirit, a will, a mind, a vital, a physical consciousness that remain resolutely turned towards the Divine and unshaken by all suggestion of doubt, desire, attachment, depression, sorrow, pain, inertia. This is possible when the

The Psychic Being and Sadhana

inner being awakens, when one becomes conscious of the Self, of the inner Mind, the inner Vital, the inner Physical, for that can more easily attune itself to the divine Will, and then there is a division in the being as if there were two beings, one within, calm, strong, equal, unperturbed, a channel of the Divine Consciousness and Force, one without still encroached on by the lower Nature; but then the disturbances of the latter become something superficial which are no more than an outer ripple, — until these under the inner pressure fade and sink away and the outer being too remains calm, concentrated, unattackable. There is also the way of the psychic, — when the psychic being comes out in its inherent power, its consecration, adoration, love of the divine, self-giving, surrender and imposes these on the mind, vital and physical consciousness and compels them to turn all their movements Godward. If the psychic is strong and master throughout, then there is no or little subjective suffering and the objective cannot affect either the soul or the other parts of the consciousness — the way is sunlit and a great joy and sweetness are the note of the whole sadhana. As for the outer attacks and adverse circumstances, that depends on the action of the Force transforming the relations of the being with the outer Nature; as the victory of the Force proceeds, they will be eliminated; but however long they last, they cannot impede the sadhana, for then even adverse things and happenings become a means for its advance and for the growth of the spirit.

Sri Aurobindo

Section V

THE AFTERLIFE AND REBIRTH

Although Death walks beside us on Life's road,
A dim bystander at the body's start
And a last judgment on man's futile works,
Other is the riddle of its ambiguous face:
Death is a stair, a door, a stumbling stride
The soul must take to cross from birth to birth,
A grey defeat pregnant with victory,
A whip to lash us towards our deathless state.
The inconscient world is the spirit's self-made room,
Eternal Night shadow of eternal Day.
Night is not our beginning nor our end;
She is the dark Mother in whose womb we have hid
Safe from too swift a waking to world-pain.
We came to her from a supernal Light,
By Light we live and to the Light we go.

Sri Aurobindo
Savitri, Book X, Canto 1

All that is made and once again unmade,
The calm persistent vision of the One
Inevitably re-makes, it lives anew:
Forces and lives and beings and ideas
Are taken into the stillness for a while;
There they remould their purpose and their drift,
Recast their nature and re-form their shape.
Ever they change and changing ever grow,
And passing through a fruitful stage of death
And after long reconstituting sleep
Resume their place in the process of the Gods
Until their work in cosmic Time is done.

Ibid., Book II, Canto XIV

The Process of Rebirth

The soul takes birth each time, and each time a mind, life and body are formed out of the materials of universal nature according to the soul's past evolution and its need for the future.

When the body is dissolved, the vital goes into the vital plane and remains there for a time, but after a time the vital sheath disappears. The last to dissolve is the mental sheath. Finally the soul or psychic being retires into the psychic world to rest there till a new birth is close.

This is the general course for ordinarily developed human beings. There are variations according to the nature of the individual and his development. For example, if the mental is strongly developed, then the mental being can remain; so also can the vital, provided they are organized by and centred around the true psychic being; they share the immortality of the psychic.

The soul gathers the essential elements of its experiences in life and makes that its basis of growth in the evolution; when it returns to birth it takes up with its mental, vital, physical sheaths so much of its Karma as is useful to it in the new life for further experience.

It is really for the vital part of the being that *śrāddha* and rites are done — to help the being to get rid of the vital vibrations which still attach it to the earth or to the vital worlds, so that it may pass quickly to its rest in the psychic peace.

Sri Aurobindo

1. The psychic being stands behind mind, life and body,

supporting them; so also the psychic world is not one world in the scale like the mental, vital or physical worlds, but stands behind all these and it is there that the souls evolving here retire for the time between life and life. If the psychic were only one principle in the rising order of body, life and mind on a par with the others and placed somewhere in the scale on the same footing as the others, it could not be the soul of all the rest, the divine element making the evolution of the others possible and using them as instruments for a growth through cosmic experience towards the Divine. So also the psychic world cannot be one among the other worlds to which the evolutionary being goes for supraphysical experience; it is a plane where it retires into itself for rest, for a spiritual assimilation of what it has experienced and for a replunging into its own fundamental consciousness and psychic nature.

2. For the few who go out of the Ignorance and enter into Nirvana, there is no question of their going straight up into higher worlds of manifestation. Nirvana or Moksha is a liberated condition of the being, not a world — it is a withdrawal from the worlds and the manifestation. The analogy of *pitṛyāna* and *devayāna* can hardly be mentioned in this connection.

3. The condition of the souls that retire into the psychic world is entirely static; each withdraws into himself and is not interacting with the others. When they come out of their trance, they are ready to go down into a new life, but meanwhile they do not act upon the earth life. There are other beings, guardians of the psychic world, but they are concerned only with the psychic world itself and the return of the souls to reincarnation, not with the earth.

The Afterlife and Rebirth

4. A being of a psychic world cannot get fused into the soul of a human being on earth. What happens in some cases is that a very advanced psychic being sometimes sends down an emanation which resides in a human being and prepares it until it is ready for the psychic being itself to enter into the life. This happens when some special work has to be done and the human vehicle prepared. Such a descent produces a remarkable change of a sudden character in the personality and the nature.

5. Usually, a soul follows continuously the same line of sex. If there are shiftings of sex, it is, as a rule, a matter of parts of the personality which are not central.

6. As regards the stage at which the soul returning for rebirth enters the new body no rule can be laid down, for the circumstances vary with the individual. Some psychic beings get into relation with the birth-environment and the parents from the time of conception and determine the preparation of the personality and future in the embryo, others join only at the time of delivery, others even later on in the life and in these cases it is some emanation of the psychic being which upholds the life. It should be noted that the conditions of the future birth are determined fundamentally not during the stay in the psychic world but at the time of death — the psychic being then chooses what it should work out in the next terrestrial appearance and the conditions arrange themselves accordingly.

Note that the idea of rebirth and the circumstances of the new life as a reward or punishment of *puṇya* or *pāpa* is a crude human idea of "justice" which is quite unphilosophical and unspiritual and distorts the true intention of life. Life here is an evolution and the soul grows by experience, working out by it this or that in the nature, and if there is suffering, it is for the purpose of that working out, not as a judgment inflicted by God or Cosmic Law on the errors or stumblings which are inevitable in the Ignorance.

SRI AUROBINDO

It is often said that children enter into possession of their psychic being when they are about seven. What does this mean exactly?

This is not correct. There are people whose psychic being watches over their formation before their birth, even before they are in the womb of their mother. There are children whose psychic being comes into contact with them at the very moment they utter their first cry. There are also people whose psychic being comes a few hours after their birth, or some days after, or some weeks, some months, some years after or... never!

THE MOTHER

I know nothing about any terrible suffering endured by the soul in the process of rebirth; popular beliefs even when they have some foundation are seldom enlightened and accurate.

SRI AUROBINDO

The psychic does not give up the mental and other sheaths (apart from the physical) immediately at death. It is said that it takes three years on the whole to get clear away from the zone of communicability with the earth — though there may

The Afterlife and Rebirth 133

be cases of slower or quicker passage. The psychic world does not communicate with earth — at any rate, not in that way. And the ghost or spirit who turns up at seances is not the psychic being. What comes through the medium is a mixture of the medium's subconscient (using subconscient in the ordinary, not in the yogic sense) and that of the sitters, vital sheaths left by the departed or perhaps occupied or used by some spirit or some vital being, the departed himself in his vital sheath or else something assumed for the occasion (but it is the vital part that communicates), elementals, spirits of the lowest vital physical world near earth, etc., etc. A horrible confusion for the most part — a hotch-potch of all sorts of things coming through a medium of "astral" grey light and shadow. Many communicants seem to be people who have just gone across into a subtle world where they feel surrounded by an improved edition of the earthly life and think that that is the real and definitive other world after earth — but it is mere optimistic prolongation of the ideas and images and associations of the human plane. Hence the next world as depicted by the spiritualist "guides" and other seance communicants.

SRI AUROBINDO

There may be what seems to be retrograde movements but these are only like zigzag movements, not a real falling back, but a return of something not worked out so as to go on better afterwards. The soul does not go back to the animal condition; but a part of the vital personality may disjoin itself and join an animal birth to work out its animal propensities there.

SRI AUROBINDO

The soul, the psychic being, once having reached the human consciousness cannot go back to the inferior animal consciousness any more than it can go back into a tree or an ephemeral insect. What is true is that some part of the vital energy or the formed instrumental consciousness or nature can and very frequently does so, if it is strongly attached to anything in the earth life. This may account for some cases of immediate rebirth with full memory in human forms also. Ordinarily, it is only by yogic development or by clairvoyance that the exact memory of past lives can be brought back.

SRI AUROBINDO

What Survives after Death and Reincarnates

This conception of the Person and Personality, if accepted, must modify at the same time our current ideas about the immortality of the soul; for, normally, when we insist on the soul's undying existence, what is meant is the survival after death of a definite unchanging personality which was and will always remain the same throughout eternity. It is the very imperfect superficial "I" of the moment, evidently regarded by Nature as a temporary form and not worth preservation, for which we demand this stupendous right to survival and immortality. But the demand is extravagant and cannot be conceded; the "I" of the moment can only merit survival if it consents to change, to be no longer itself but something else, greater, better, more luminous in knowledge, more moulded in the image of the eternal inner beauty, more and more progressive towards the divinity of the secret Spirit. It is that secret Spirit or divinity of Self in us which is imperishable, because it is unborn and eternal. The psychic entity within, its representative, the spiritual individual in us, is the Person that we are; but the "I" of this moment, the "I" of this life is only a formation, a temporary personality of this inner Person: it is one step of the many steps of our evolutionary change, and it serves its true purpose only when we pass beyond it to a farther step leading nearer to a higher degree of consciousness and being. It is the inner Person that survives death, even as it pre-exists before birth; for this constant survival is a rendering of the eternity of our timeless Spirit into the terms of Time.

SRI AUROBINDO

You must avoid a common popular blunder about reincarnation. The popular idea is that Titus Balbus is reborn again as John Smith, a man with the same personality, character, attainments as he had in his former life with the sole difference that he wears coat and trousers instead of a toga and speaks in cockney English instead of popular Latin. That is not the case. What would be the earthly use of repeating the same personality or character a million times from the beginning of time till its end? The soul comes into birth for experience, for growth, for evolution till it can bring the Divine into Matter. It is the central being that incarnates, not the outer personality — the personality is simply a mould that it creates for its figures of experience in that one life. In another birth it will create for itself a different personality, different capacities, a different life and career. Supposing Virgil is born again, he may take up poetry in one or two other lives, but he will certainly not write an epic but rather perhaps slight but elegant and beautiful lyrics such as he wanted to write, but did not succeed, in Rome. In another birth he is likely to be no poet at all, but a philosopher and a yogin seeking to attain and to express the highest truth — for that too was an unrealised trend of his consciousness in that life. Perhaps before he had been a warrior or ruler doing deeds like Aeneas or Augustus before he sang them. And so on — on this side or that the central being develops a new character, a new personality, grows, develops, passes through all kinds of terrestrial experience.

As the evolving being develops still more and becomes more rich and complex, it accumulates its personalities, as it were. Sometimes they stand behind the active elements, throwing in some colour, some trait, some capacity here and there, — or they stand in front and there is a multiple personality, a many-sided character or a many-sided, sometimes what looks like a universal capacity. But if a former personality, a former capacity is brought fully forward, it will not be to repeat what was already done, but to cast the same capacity into new forms and new shapes and fuse it into a new harmony of the being which will not be a reproduction of what was before. Thus you must not expect to be what the warrior and the poet were. Something of the outer characteristics may reappear but very much changed and new-cast in a new combination. It is in a new direction that the energies will be guided to do what was not done before.

Another thing. It is not the personality, the character that is of the first importance in rebirth — it is the psychic being who stands behind the evolution of the nature and evolves with it. The psychic when it departs from the body, shedding even the mental and vital on its way to its resting place, carries with it the heart of its experiences, — not the physical events, not the vital movements, not the mental buildings, not the capacities or characters, but something essential that it gathered from them, what might be called the divine element for the sake of which the rest existed. That is the permanent addition, it is that that helps in the growth towards the Divine. That is why there is usually no memory of the outward events and circumstances of past lives — for this memory there must be a strong development towards unbroken continuance of the mind, the vital, even the subtle physical; for though it all remains in a kind of seed memory, it does not ordinarily emerge. What was the divine element in the magnanimity of the warrior, that which expressed itself in his loyalty, nobility, high courage, what was the divine element behind the harmonious mentality and generous vitality of the poet and expressed itself in them, that remains and in a new harmony of character may find a new expression or, if the life is turned towards the Divine, be taken up as powers for the realisation or for the work that has to be done for the Divine.

SRI AUROBINDO

The Psychic's Choice and Conditions of Rebirth

The psychic being at the time of death chooses what it will work out in the next birth and determines the character and conditions of the new personality. Life is for the evolutionary growth by experience in the conditions of the Ignorance till one is ready for the higher Light.

SRI AUROBINDO

The dying wish of the man is only something on the surface — it may be determined by the psychic and so help to shape the future but it does not determine the psychic's choice. That is something behind the veil. It is not the outer consciousness's action that determines the inner process, but the other way round. Sometimes, however, there are signs or fragments of the inner action that come up on the surface, e.g. some people have a vision or remembrance of the circumstances of their past in a panoramic flash at the time of death, that is the psychic's review of the life before departing.

SRI AUROBINDO

The psychic being's choice at the time of death does not *work out* the next formation of personality, it *fixes* it. When it enters the psychic world, it begins to assimilate the essence of its experience and by that assimilation is formed the future psychic personality in accordance with the fixation already made. When this assimilation is over, it is ready for a new birth; but the less developed beings do not work out the whole thing for themselves, there are beings and forces of the higher world who have that work. Also, when it comes to birth, it is not sure that the forces of the physical world will not come across the working out of what it wanted — its own new instrumentation may not be strong enough for that purpose; for, there is the interaction of its own energies and the cosmic forces here. There may be frustration, diversion, a partial working out — many things may happen. All that is not a rigid machinery, it is a working out of complex forces. It may be added, however, that a developed psychic being is much more conscious in this transition and works out much

The Afterlife and Rebirth

of it itself. The time depends also on the development and on a certain rhythm of the being — for some there is practically immediate rebirth, for others it takes longer, for some it may take centuries; but here, again, once the psychic being is sufficiently developed, it is free to choose its own rhythm and its own intervals. The ordinary theories are too mechanical — and that is the case also with the idea of *puṇya* and *pāpa* and their results in the next life. There are certainly results of the energies put forth in a past life, but not on that rather infantile principle. A good man's suffering in this life would be a proof according to the orthodox theory that he had been a very great villain in his past life, a bad man's prospering would be a proof that he had been quite angelic in his last visit to earth and sown a large crop of virtues and meritorious actions to reap this bumper crop of good fortune. Too symmetrical to be true. The object of birth being growth by experience, whatever reactions come to past deeds must be for the being to learn and grow, not as lollipops for good boys of the class (in the past) and canings for the bad ones. The real sanction for good and ill is not good fortune for the one and bad fortune for the other, but this that good leads us towards a higher nature which is eventually lifted above suffering, and ill pulls us towards the lower nature which remains always in the circle of suffering and evil.

SRI AUROBINDO

For the destiny which follows after death, the last state of consciousness is usually the most important. That is, if at the moment of death one has the intense aspiration to return to continue his work, then the conditions are arranged for it to be done. But, you see, there are all the possibilities, for what happens after death. There are people who return in the psychic. You see, I have told you that the outer being is very rarely preserved; so we speak only of the psychic consciousness which, indeed, always persists. And then there are people for whom the psychic returns to the psychic domain to assimilate the experience they have had and to prepare their future life. This may take centuries, it depends on the people.

The more evolved the psychic is, the nearer it is to its complete maturity, the greater the time between the births. There are beings who reincarnate only after a thousand years, two thousand years.

The closer one is to the beginning of the formation, the closer are the reincarnations; and sometimes even, altogether at the lower level, when man is quite near the animal, it goes like this (*gesture*), that is, it is not unusual for people to reincarnate in the children of their children, like that, something like that, or just in the next generation. But this is always on a very primitive level of evolution, and the psychic being is not very conscious, it is in the state of formation. And as it becomes more developed, the reincarnations, as I said, are at a greater distance from one another. When the psychic being is fully developed, when it no longer needs to return to earth for its development, when it is absolutely free, it has the choice between no longer coming back to earth if it finds that its work lies elsewhere or if it prefers to remain in the purely psychic consciousness, without reincarnating; or else it can come when it wants, as it wants, where it wants, perfectly consciously. And there are those who have united with forces of a universal order and with entities of the Overmind or

The Afterlife and Rebirth

elsewhere, who remain all the time in the earth atmosphere and take on bodies successively for the work. This means that the moment the psychic being is completely formed and absolutely free — when it is completely formed it becomes absolutely free — it can do anything it likes, it depends on what it chooses; therefore one can't say, "It will be like this, it will be like that"; it does exactly what it wants and it can even announce (that has happened), at the moment of the death of the body, what its next reincarnation will be and what it will do, and already choose what it is going to do. But before this state, which is not very frequent — it depends absolutely on the degree of development of the psychic and the hope formulated by the integral consciousness of the being — there is still the mental, vital and physical consciousness, united with the psychic consciousness; so at that moment, the moment of death, the moment of leaving the body, it formulates a hope or an aspiration or a will, and usually this decides the future life.

THE MOTHER

Can it happen that the psychic being does not fall at the place where it wanted to take birth?

If a psychic being sees from its psychic world a light on the earth, it may rush down there without knowing exactly where it is. Everything is possible. But if the psychic being is very conscious, sufficiently conscious, it will seek the light of aspiration in a precise place, because of the culture, the education it will find there. This happens much more frequently than one believes, especially in somewhat educated circles.

An intelligent woman with some artistic or philosophical culture, a beginning of conscious individuality, may aspire that the child she is going to have may be the best possible according to her idea or according to what she has read. Hence it is not so very complicated to find a place. The number of psychic beings born constantly being considerable, if each time exceptional conditions have to be found it would be difficult. Surely, there are instances where the psychic being seems to have fallen headlong and been stunned, but this is bad luck; in such a case it generally requires a long time to wake up. It is bad luck in the sense that it probably lacked a certain power of discrimination, or perhaps it had to face certain forces which thwarted its decision and won a partial victory over it. There are a thousand possibilities, you know. One cannot say that everything goes according to the same plan — every psychic being is different.

THE MOTHER

For past lives, are there any general rules, broad outlines, or is everything possible?

All depends on the category to which one belongs, and the degree of the psychic being's development. If the psychic being is in an advanced stage, near maturity, the choice before death... is quite real and this choice means that everything is possible; but in other cases, the rebirth takes place almost automatically. The will of the psychic being is not developed and it does not choose. Hence, there are no rules. It depends very much on circumstances, and especially on the line of formation which the psychic being will follow,

The Afterlife and Rebirth

and that depends on its origin. It is difficult to say. In the matter of sex, that may vary for a long time. As the consciousness grows and gains some unity of action, of consciousness, it can choose to follow one line to the exclusion of another, but before this choice, through innumerable creations you have been undoubtedly of different sexes. That is why perhaps some women have a masculine character, and vice versa, or have tendencies opposite to their sex. But at the time of the "choice" one may decide to belong to the creatrix Consciousness or to the immobile Witness. That depends upon the origin.

THE MOTHER

When the psychic is about to enter into the world, does it choose in advance the form it is going to take?

It is an interesting question. That depends…. There are psychic beings who are in the making, on the way to progress; these generally, right at the outset, cannot choose much, but when they have arrived at a certain degree of growth and of consciousness (generally while they are still in a physical body and have had a certain amount of experience), they decide at that time what their next field of experience will be like.

I can give you some rather external examples. For instance, a psychic being needed to have the experience of mastery, of power in order to know the reactions and how it is possible to turn all these movements towards the Divine: to learn what a life of power may teach you. It took birth in a king or a queen. These enjoyed some power and during that time they had their experiences; they reached the end of the field of experience. Now, they know what they wanted to know, they are about to go, they are going to leave their body that's now become useless, and they are going to prepare for the next experience. Well, at that time, when the psychic being is still in the body and has noted what it has learnt, it decides for the next occasion. And sometimes it is a movement of action and reaction: because it has studied one entire field, it needs to study the opposite field. And very often it chooses a very different life from the one it had. So before leaving, it says: "Next time, it is in this domain that I shall take birth...." Suppose, for example, the psychic has reached a stage of growth when it would like to have the chance of working on the physical body to make it capable of coming consciously into contact with the Divine and of transforming it. Now, it is about to leave the body in which it had authority, power, activity, the body it has used for its growth; it says: "Next time I shall take birth in a neutral environment, neither low nor high, where it will not be necessary (how to put it?) to have a highly external life, where one will have neither great power not great misery — altogether neutral, as you know, the life in between." It chooses that. It returns to its own psychic world for the necessary rest, for assimilation of the experience gained, for preparation of the future experience. It naturally remembers its choice and, before coming down once more, when it has finished its assimilation, when it is time to return, to come down upon earth, it cannot, from that domain, see material things as we see them, you know: they appear to it in another form. But still the differences can be foreseen: the differences of envi-

The Afterlife and Rebirth

ronment, differences of activity in the environment are clearly seen, quite perceptible. It can have a vision that is total or global. It can choose. At times it chooses the country; when it wants a certain kind of education, civilisation, influence, it can choose its country beforehand. Sometimes it can't, sometimes it chooses only its environment and the kind of life it will lead. And then from up there, before it comes down, it looks for the kind of vibrations it wants; it sees them very clearly. It is as though it was aiming at the place where it is going to drop. But it is an approximation because of the fact that another condition is necessary: not only its choice but also a receptivity from below and an aspiration. There must be someone in the environment it has chosen, generally the mother (something both the parents, but the most indispensable is the mother), she must have an aspiration or a receptivity, something sufficiently passive and open or a conscious aspiration towards something higher. And that kindles for the psychic being a little light. In the mass representing for it the environment in which it wants to be born, if under the influence of its own projected will a small light is kindled, then it knows that it is there it must go.

It is necessary, it is this that makes the difference in months or days, perhaps, not so much perhaps in years; however, this creates an uncertainty, and that is why it cannot foretell the exact date: "On that date, that day, at that hour I shall take birth." It needs to find someone receptive. When it sees that, it rushes down. But what happens is something like an image: it is not exactly that, but something very similar. It throws itself down into an unconsciousness, because the physical world, even human consciousness whatever it may be, is very unconscious in comparison with the psychic consciousness. So it rushes into an unconsciousness. It is as though it fell head foremost. That stuns it. And so generally, apart from some very very rare exceptions, for a long time it does not know. It does not know any longer where it is nor what it is doing nor why it is there, nothing at all. It finds a great difficulty in expressing itself, especially through a baby that has no brain, naturally; it is only the embryo of a brain which is hardly formed and it does not have the elements for manifesting itself. So it is very rare for a child to manifest immediately the exceptional being it contains.... That happens. Such things we have heard being narrated. It happens, but generally some time is needed. Only slowly it awakens from its stupor and becomes aware that it is there for some reason and by choice. And usually this coincides with the intensive mental education which shuts you completely from the psychic consciousness. So a mass of circumstances, happenings of all kinds, emotions, all sorts of things are necessary to open the inner doors so that one might begin to remember that after all one has come from another world and one has come for a precise reason.

Otherwise, if all went normally, it could very quickly have a connection, very quickly. If it had the luck to find someone possessing a little knowledge, and instead of falling into a world of ignorance, it fell upon a little bit of knowledge, everything would be done quite quickly.

THE MOTHER

When great souls want to be born upon earth, do they choose their parents?

The Afterlife and Rebirth

Ah! That depends on their state of consciousness, it depends on the state of their psychic formation. If the psychic being is completely formed, if it has reached the perfection of its being and is free to reincarnate or not, it has also the capacity of choosing.... They don't have a physical sight like ours so long as they are not in a body. So, evidently, they look for a body which is adapted and fit to express them, but they must give its share to the material inconscience, if it may be put thus, and to the necessity to adapt themselves to the most material laws of the body. So, from the point of view of the psychic, the choice of the place where one is born is important, it is more than an insignificant detail. But there are so many things that can't be foreseen. For instance, one chooses an environment, a country, a certain type of family, one tries to see the nature of the probable parents, one asks for certain already well-developed qualities in them and a sufficient self-mastery. But all this is not enough if one does not carry in oneself a sufficient dynamism to overcome the obstacles. So, all things considered, this is not enormously important. Anyhow, even at the best, even if the parents have collaborated consciously, there is an enormous mass of the subconscient and the yet lower inconscient which from time to time rises again to the surface, gets stirred up, damages the work, makes calmness and silence indispensable. Always, always a preparation is needed, even if one has chosen — a long preparation. Not to speak of the phenomenon of being half-stunned at the moment of birth, the descent into the body, which often lasts for a very long time before one can escape from it completely.

THE MOTHER

The formation of the body depends entirely on a man and a woman, but is the soul which manifests in the child, in the body which is being formed, compelled to manifest in this body?

You mean whether it can choose between different bodies?

Yes.

Well, it is very exceptional, after all, in the great mass of humanity, that a conscious soul incarnates voluntarily. It is something very unusual. I have already told you that when a soul is conscious, fully formed, and wants to incarnate, usually from its psychic plane it looks for a corresponding psychic light at a certain place upon earth. Besides, during its previous incarnation, before going away, before leaving the earth-atmosphere, usually as a result of the experience it had in the life that is coming to an end, the soul chooses more or less — not in all details but broadly — the conditions of its future life. But these are exceptional cases. Possibly we could speak of it for ourselves here, but for the majority, the vast majority of men, even those who are educated, it is out of the question. And what comes then is a psychic being in formation, more or less formed, and there are all the stages of formation from the spark which becomes a little light to the fully formed being, and this extends over thousands of years. This ascent of the soul to become a conscious being having its own will, capable of determining the choice of its own life, takes thousands of years.

So, you are thinking of a soul which would say, "No, I refuse this body, I am going to look for another"?... I don't

The Afterlife and Rebirth 149

say it is impossible — everything is possible. It does happen, in fact, that children are still-born, which means that there was no soul to incarnate in them. But it may be for other reasons also; it may be for reasons of malformation only; one can't say. I don't say it is impossible, but generally, when a conscious and free soul chooses to take a body on earth again, even before its birth it works on this body. So it has no reason not to accept even the inconveniences which may result from the ignorance of the parents; for it has chosen the place for a reason which was not one of ignorance: it saw a light there — it might have been simply the light of a possibility, but there was a light and *that is why* it has come there. So, it is all very well to say, "Ah! No, I don't like it", but where would it go to choose another it likes?... That may happen, I don't say it is impossible, but it cannot happen very often. For, when from the psychic plane the soul looks at the earth and chooses the place for its next birth, it chooses it with sufficient discernment not to be altogether grossly mistaken.

It has also happened that souls have incarnated and then left. There are many reasons why they go away. Children who die very young, after a few days or a few weeks — this may be for a similar reason. Most often it is said that the soul needed just a little experience to complete its formation, that it had it during these few weeks and then left. Everything is possible. And as many stories would be needed to tell the story of souls as are needed to tell the story of men. That is to say, they are innumerable and the instances are as different as possible from one another.

So, to decide arbitrarily: "It is like that, not like this; this is what happens and not that", this is childishness. *Every-*

thing can happen. There are instances which occur more frequently than others, one can generalise, but one can never say, "This is not possible and it is always like this or always like that." That is not how things happen.

But anyway — anyway — even in the best cases, even when the soul has come consciously, even when it has consciously participated in the formation of the physical body, still so long as the body is formed in the usual animal way, it will have to struggle and correct all those things which come from this human animality.

Inevitably, parents have a particular formation, they are particularly healthy or unhealthy; even taking things at their best, they have a heap of atavisms, habits, formations in the subconscious and even in the unconscious, which come from their own birth, the environment they have lived in, their own life; and even if they are remarkable people, they have a large number of things which are quite opposed to the true psychic life — even the best of them, even the most conscious. And besides, there is all that is going to happen. Even if one takes a great deal of trouble over the education of one's children, they will come in contact with all sorts of people who will have an influence over them, especially when they are very young, and these influences enter the subconscious, one has to struggle against them later on. I say: even in the best cases, because of the way in which the body is formed at present, you have to face innumerable difficulties which come more or less from the subconscious, but rise to the surface and against which you have to struggle before you can become completely free and develop normally.

THE MOTHER

Memory of Past Lives

The departed soul retains the memory of its past experiences only in their essence, not in their form of detail. It is only if the soul brings back some past personality or personalities as part of its present manifestation that it is likely to remember the details of the past life. Otherwise, it is only by Yogadrishti that the memory comes.

SRI AUROBINDO

In rebirth it is not the external being, that which is formed by parents, environment and circumstances — the mental, the vital and the physical — that is born again: it is only the psychic being that passes from body to body. Logically, then, neither the mental nor the vital being can remember past lives or recognise itself in the character or mode of life of this or that person. The psychic being alone can remember; and it is by becoming conscious of our psychic being that we can have at the same time exact impressions about our past lives.

THE MOTHER

In ordinary lives — and by that I mean the life of a certain *élite* of sufficiently well-developed people — the contact between the external being and the psychic is quite intermittent; it is the result of certain experiences or certain inner needs. At that moment the psychic being is "in front", as Sri Aurobindo says, that is, it comes to the surface of the consciousness, it is in direct contact with material circumstances, with forms and words and sounds, etc., for a very short time; so it records all that like a photograph or a cinema, but it is just a minute, a few moments in a lifetime. These moments may repeat themselves several times, but they do not last; and it is this the psychic being remembers; and when you have real psychic memories, sincere, spontaneous, not fabricated by the mind or the vital, that is, purely psychic, exact, your memory is *intermittent*. And it is often very difficult to locate your past lives, to say: "I was this or that." It is only when the psychic experience has taken place at a very important moment of your life and a whole set of circumstances gives you, so to say, the key to the story (dresses, spoken words, customs or an environment giving you the key) that you can say: "Oh! that life, I have lived it." But if someone comes and narrates to you all his previous lives from the monkey onwards, with a mass of details, you may be sure that he is a humbug!

THE MOTHER

How is it that in newspapers one quite often reads stories of small children who remember their past lives and that the details have been verified? And it is the study of such events that leads parapsychologists to assert the existence of reincarnation. So are they not on a completely wrong track? And how can reincarnation be demonstrated scientifically in any other way?

The memories you refer to, which are mentioned in newspapers, are memories of the vital being that, exceptionally, has gone out of one body in order to enter another. It is something that can happen, but it is not frequent.

The memory that I refer to is that of the psychic being,

The Afterlife and Rebirth

and one is conscious of it only when one is in conscious relation with one's psychic being.

There is no contradiction between the two things.

THE MOTHER

In nine hundred and ninety-nine cases out of a thousand, it is just the tiny psychic formation at the centre of the being that continues after death; all the rest is dissolved, goes to pieces, scattered here and there, the individuality exists no longer. Now, how often in the physical life does the psychic being take part consciously in what the physical being does?... I am not speaking of people who do yoga and are a little disciplined; I am speaking of average people who have a psychic capacity in the sense that their psychic is already sufficiently developed to be able to intervene in life and guide it — some pass years and years without the psychic intervening. And they come and tell you in which country they were born and what their father and mother were like and the house they lived in, the roof of the church and the forest that was by the side and all the most casual events of their life! It is absolutely idiotic, for it is all rubbed off, these things don't exist any longer; whilst the memory that one may still have is that of the particular moment in life when there is a special circumstance, "vital" moments, so to say, in which the psychic suddenly takes part, through an inner call or an absolute necessity — all of a sudden the psychic intervenes — and that then is engraved in the psychic memory. When you have the psychic memory you remember a set of circumstances at one *moment* of life, particularly of the inner emotion, of the consciousness that acted at that moment. And then that passes into the consciousness along with some associations, with all that was around you, perhaps a word spoken, a phrase heard; but what was most important was the state of the soul in which you were: for that indeed remains very clearly engraved. These are the landmarks of the psychic life, things that have left a deep impression and taken part in its formation. Hence when you find your psychic being in you again constantly, continuously, clearly, it is things like these that you remember. There may be quite a few, but they are flashes in one's life, and one cannot say: "I was such and such a person, I did such and such a thing, I was called by this name and I was doing this or that." Or otherwise it would mean that at that moment (a rare one) there was a combination of circumstances good enough for one to be able to fix the date or the place, the country and the age. That can happen.

Naturally the psychic takes a greater and greater part, and the larger does the set of memories grow. And then one can retrace one's life, but not in all its details. One can say that at certain moments, "it was like this," or "I was that." Certain moments, yes, very important moments of a life.... What's necessary is a being wholly identified with the psychic, one that has organised its whole existence around it, unified its whole being — all the tiniest parts, all the elements, all the movements of the being around the psychic centre — that has made of itself a single being, solely turned to the Divine; then, if the body falls off, that remains. It is only a completely formed conscious being that can remember exactly in another life all that has happened before. It can even pass consciously from one life to another without losing anything of its consciousness. How many people upon earth have reached that state?... Not many, I believe. And usually they are not in the least inclined to narrate their adventures.

THE MOTHER

Only when one is consciously identified with one's divine origin, can one in truth speak of a memory of past lives. Sri Aurobindo speaks of the progressive manifestation of the Spirit in the forms in which it dwells. When one reaches the summit of this manifestation, one has a vision that plunges down upon the way traversed and one remembers.

But this memory is not a thing of the mental kind. Those who claim to have been such a baron of the Middle Ages or such a person who lived at such a place and such a time, are fanciful, they are simply victims of their own mental imagination. In fact, what remains of past lives are not beautiful pictures in which you appear as a mighty lord in a castle or a victorious general at the head of an army — that is only romance. What remains is the memory of those instants when the psychic being emerged from the depths of your being and revealed itself to you — that is to say, the memory of those instants when you were wholly conscious. That growth of consciousness is progressively effectuated in the course of evolution, and the memory of past lives is generally limited to the critical moments of evolution, to the decisive turns that marked the progress of your consciousness.

At the time when you live such moments of your life, you do not care at all about remembering that you were Mr. X, such a person, living at such a place and in such an epoch; it is not the memory of your civic status that remains. On the contrary, you lose all consciousness of these petty external things, accessories and perishables, so that you may be wholly in the flare of the soul revelation or of the divine contact. When you remember such instants of your past lives, the memory is so intense that it seems to be still very close, still living, and much more living than most of the ordinary memories of our present life. At times, in dreams, when you come into contact with certain planes of consciousness, you may have memories of such intensity, such vibrant colour, so to say, even more intense than the colours and things of the physical world. For these are the moments of true consciousness, and everything then puts on an extraordinary brilliance, everything is vibrant, everything is imbued with a quality that escapes the ordinary eye.

These minutes of contact with the soul are often those that mark a decisive turn of our life, a forward step, a progress in consciousness, and that frequently corresponds with a crisis, an extremely intense situation when there comes a call in the whole being, a call so strong that the inner consciousness pierces the layers of unconsciousness covering it and is revealed all luminous on the surface. This call of the being, when very strong, can also bring about the descent of a divine emanation, an individuality, a divine aspect which joins with your individuality at a given moment in order to do a given work, win a battle, express one thing or another. The work done, the emanation very often withdraws. Then one may retain the memory of the circumstances that were around those minutes of revelation or inspiration: one sees again the scenery, the colour of the dress that one had put on, the colour of one's own skin, the things about you at that time — all that is fixed indelibly with an extraordinary intensity,

The Afterlife and Rebirth

because the things of the ordinary life revealed themselves then in their true intensity and their true colour. The consciousness that reveals itself in you, reveals at the same time the consciousness that is in things. At times, with the help of these details you may reconstitute the age in which you lived or the action that you did, find out the country where you were; but it is very easy also to make a romance and take imagination for reality.

Yet you must not believe that all memories of past lives are those of moments of great crisis, of important mission or of revelation. Sometimes they are moments very simple, transparent, when an integral, a perfect harmony of the being was expressed. And that may correspond to altogether insignificant external situations.

Apart from the things that were in your immediate surrounding at that moment, apart from that moment of contact with your psychic being, nothing remains. Once the privileged moment passes, the psychic being plunges into an inner somnolence and the whole outer life melts into a grey monotony which does not leave any trace. Besides, it is almost the same phenomenon as what happens in the course of the life that you lead at present: apart from those exceptional moments when you are at the summit of your being, mental or vital or even physical, the rest of your life seems to melt into a kind of neutral colour which has no great interest, when it matters little whether you were at such a place instead of being at another, whether you did this thing or that. If you try to look at your life all at once, in order to gather, as it were, its essence, the twenty or thirty or forty years behind you, you will see rise up spontaneously two or three images which were the true moments of your life; the rest is effaced. A kind of spontaneous choice works in your consciousness and there is a tremendous elimination. This will give you a little idea of what happens in regard to past lives: the choice of a few select moments and an immense elimination.

It is very true that the earliest lives are very rudimentary; very few things subsist out of that, scattered memories few and far between. But the more one progresses in consciousness, the more the psychic being is consciously associated with the outer activities; the memories grow in number and become more coherent and precise. But still, here also, the memory that remains is that of the contact with the soul and at times that of things which were associated with the psychic revelation — not the civic status or the changing scenes around. And this will explain to you why the so-called memories of past animal lives are the most fantastic: the divine spark in them is buried much too deep down to be able to come up consciously to the surface and be associated with the outer life. One must become a wholly conscious being, conscious in all its parts, totally united with one's divine origin before one can truly say that one remembers his past lives.

THE MOTHER

There are people who tell the life of others.

Yes, I know. I know many things, I have heard all that one can hear. They tell stories after stories.... They look at you and say: "You were so-and-so in that life, you did such and such a thing." Well, I guarantee, it is not true. For I know how one can find out where one has seen a person and what

The Afterlife and Rebirth

he was and how it is — it is not just a little story that you can write in a book. When you look within a person, when you have the perception, precisely of the psychic world, which enables you to recognise the psychic there where it was, then all of a sudden you can see a scene, an image, a form, a word; there is a sort of association due to which even in the present being of this person there still remain certain sympathies and attractions which come from previous lives. But, as I was saying, these are "moments" of life. And so one sees, one can see these various moments, but one cannot narrate a whole life.

THE MOTHER

Section VI

MORE LIGHTS ON THE PSYCHIC BEING

A conscious soul in the Inconscient's world,
Hidden behind our thoughts and hopes and dreams,
An indifferent Master signing Nature's acts
Leaves the vicegerent mind a seeming king.
In his floating house upon the sea of Time
The regent sits at work and never rests:
He is a puppet of the dance of Time;
He is driven by the hours, the moment's call
Compels him with the thronging of life's need
And the babel of the voices of the world.

SRI AUROBINDO
Savitri, Book VII, Canto II

More Lights on the Psychic Being

I did not understand the explanation of the psychic you have given: "One could say, for example, that the creation of an individual being is the result of the projection, in time and space, of one of the countless possibilities latent in the supreme origin of all manifestation which, through the medium of the one and universal consciousness, takes concrete form in the law or the truth of an individual and so, by a progressive development, becomes his soul or psychic being."

It is a little philosophical.... You know the difference between what is subjective and what is objective? You know it! Well, imagine precisely this Reality we were speaking about, which is at the origin of all things, passing from the subjective to the objective state. That is, what was within becomes as though projected outside. It is the *same* thing: it is the state that changes. And so, within it there are all the possibilities of objective existence; within they are unexpressed, unmanifested; outside they are projected, as a picture is projected on the cinema-screen: we see it before us. And every element that was a possibility within, a law, becomes the law of a realisation. And every one of these possibilities becomes the reality of a being, of an individuality if you like, of something existing objectively. And it is that law which is the origin of the centre of the psychic being: it is the truth of the being or the law of the being. The Buddha called it the "law", he spoke of the *Dharma*. It is the truth of the being. It is that which binds it again indestructibly to its origin. And that is the starting-point of the psychic being. And so, even as this develops, like the picture on the screen, it takes a more and more complex and precise form in the manifestation. But the reality of that form is one, it is bound to the One. And all the units are linked together and reproduce the One.

THE MOTHER

Sweet Mother, is there a spiritual being in everybody?

That depends on what we call "being". If for "being" we substitute "presence", yes, there is a spiritual presence in everyone. If we call "being" an organised entity, fully conscious of itself, independent, and having the power of asserting itself and ruling the rest of the nature — no! The possibility of this independent and all-powerful being is in everybody, but the realisation is the result of long efforts which sometimes extend over many lives.

In everyone, even at the very beginning, this spiritual presence, this inner light is there.... In fact, it is everywhere. I have seen it many a time in certain animals. It is like a shining point which is the basis of a certain control and protection, something which, even in half-consciousness, makes possible a certain harmony with the rest of creation so that irreparable catastrophes may not be constant and general. Without this presence the disorder created by the violences and passions of the vital would be so great that at any moment they could bring about a general catastrophe, a sort of total destruction which would prevent the progress of Nature. That presence, that spiritual light — which could almost be called a spiritual consciousness — is within each being and all things, and because of it, in spite of all discord-

More Lights on the Psychic Being

ance, all passion, all violence, there is a minimum of general harmony which allows Nature's work to be accomplished.

And this presence becomes quite obvious in the human being, even the most rudimentary. Even in the most monstrous human being, in one who gives the impression of being an incarnation of a devil or a monster, there is something within exercising a sort of irresistible control — even in the worst, some things are impossible. And without this presence, if the being were controlled exclusively by the adverse forces, the forces of the vital, this impossibility would not exist.

Each time a wave of these monstrous adverse forces sweeps over the earth, one feels that nothing can ever stop the disorder and horror from spreading, and always, at a certain time, unexpectedly and inexplicably a control intervenes, and the wave is arrested, the catastrophe is not total. And this is because of the Presence, the supreme Presence, in matter.

But only in a few exceptional beings and after a long, very long work of preparation extending over many, many lives does this Presence change into a conscious, independent, fully organised being, all-powerful master of his dwelling-place, conscious enough, powerful enough, to be able to control not only this dwelling but what surrounds it and in a field of radiation and action that is more and more extensive... and effective.

THE MOTHER

What characterises the substance of the psychic world?

The substance of the psychic world is a substance proper to it, with its own psychic characteristics: a sense of immortality, a complete receptivity to the divine influence, an entire submission to this influence by which it is wholly impregnated. It is this exactly which distinguishes the psychic from the other parts of the being. When, for instance, I speak of organising the mind and the vital around the psychic centre, I do not mean that they become psychic; they remain the mind and the vital, but they are organised around the psychic as an army is organised around its leader — it does not become the leader, it obeys him, doesn't it? Well, it is the same thing here; the vital and the mind are organised around the psychic, they receive orders from the psychic and carry them out as well as they can. But their substance does not become psychic substance as a consequence. They can be under the influence of the psychic and assume its nature more or less but not its substance.

THE MOTHER

Is the psychic being in the heart?

Not in the physical heart, not in the organ. It is in a fourth dimension, an inner dimension. But it is in that region, the region somewhat behind the solar plexus, it is there that one finds it most easily. The psychic being is in the fourth dimension as related to our physical being.

THE MOTHER

The psychic being is in the heart centre in the middle of the chest (not in the physical heart, for all the centres are in the middle of the body), but it is deep behind. When one is going away from the vital into the psychic, it is felt as if one

More Lights on the Psychic Being

is going deep deep down till one reaches that central place of the psychic. The surface of the heart centre is the place of the emotional being; from there one goes deep to find the psychic.

SRI AUROBINDO

The other day I said that most of the time people do not have their psychic being within them. I would like to explain this in greater detail.... You must remember that the inner beings are not in the third dimension. If you open up your body you will find only the viscera of the body which are in the third dimension. The inner beings are in another dimension, and when I say that some men do not have their psychic being within them, I do not mean that it is not at the centre of their being, but that their outer consciousness is so small, so limited, so obscure that it is not able to keep a contact, not only conscious but intimate, with the psychic being which extends beyond it in every way; it is so much higher and deeper than the other outer consciousness that there is no relation either of quality or of nature between them. Religions say that you have a divine spark in you — it is well they call it a "spark", for it is so small indeed that it can be placed anywhere in the body without difficulty. But this does not mean that it is in the body: it is within the consciousness in another dimension, and there are beings who have a contact with it, others who haven't. But if you come to the divine Presence in the atom, the image is easier to understand, for there you touch so infinitesimal a domain that you are on the borderline where you can no longer distinguish between two, three, four or five dimensions. If you study modern physics you will understand what I mean.

The movements constituting an atom are, in the matter of size, so imperceptible that they cannot be understood with our three-dimensional understanding, the more so as they follow laws which elude completely this three-dimensional idea. So if you take refuge there, you may say that the divine spark is at the centre of each atom and you won't be far from the truth; but I was not speaking of the divine spark, I was speaking of the being, the psychic consciousness, which is another thing. The psychic being is an entity which has a form; it is organised around a central consciousness and, having a form it has a dimension, but a dimension of another kind than the third dimension of the outer consciousness.

THE MOTHER

The physical heart is in the left side, but the heart centre of yoga is in the middle of the chest — the cardiac centre.

SRI AUROBINDO

I never heard of two lotuses in the heart centre; but it is the seat of two powers, in front the higher vital or emotional being, behind and concealed the soul or psychic being.

SRI AUROBINDO

The apex of the psychic and emotional centre (like the apex of all centres) is in the backbone, the base in front in middle of the sternum.

SRI AUROBINDO

The heart is the centre of the being and commands the rest, as the psychic being or *caitya puruṣa* is there. It is only in that sense that all flows from it, for it is the psychic being who each time creates a new mind, vital and body for himself.

SRI AUROBINDO

The psychic being (which is the soul) does not make centres for itself in the Adhar. The centres are there. The psychic being can take control of the centres that are already there — the heart and the navel centre and the two below the navel. Also the mind and vital are not abolished — they are brought under the psychic influence and psychicised, or they are occupied by the higher consciousness from above and transformed into its instruments.

SRI AUROBINDO

Is there a psychic being in the atom?

No, it is not yet there. It can be said that there is a possibility of psychic consciousness in Matter — the diffusion of the divine Consciousness had only one object: to make possible an organisation which would be under the direct influence of the Divine. That is why it passes over all the worlds of disorder.* It may hence be said that the Origin of the soul is also

---

* At the time of the publication of this talk, Mother added the following note for the sake of precision: "Some parts of the vital are worlds of disorder and the beings inhabiting the vital have no psychic being. The psychic being exists only upon earth, in the physical world. That is why I said in brief that the divine spark, which organises the psychic, passed over the worlds of disorder and manifested itself directly in the physical world to create there this possibility of organisation around the divine spark."

in the atom, in all the elements constituting the atom, but it is only the Origin.... I must tell you that when it is fully formed, the psychic being has a distinct form which corresponds to our physical form. It is not altogether similar, but it has a definite form. Every psychic being is different from another — they are not all cut out, modelled to one pattern. They are different, each has an individuality, a personality.

THE MOTHER

I have noticed a first rudiment of the psychic presence and vibration in vegetable life, and truly this blossoming one calls a flower is the first manifestation of the psychic presence. The psychic is individualised only in man, but it was there before him; but it is not the same kind of individualisation as in man, it is more fluid: it manifests as force, as consciousness rather than as individuality. Take the rose, for example; its great perfection of form, colour, scent expresses an aspiration and a psychic giving. Look at a rose opening in the morning at the first touch of the sun, it is a magnificent self-giving in aspiration.

THE MOTHER

Yes, it is a more simple and honest consciousness — that of the animal. Of course it expects something, but even if it does not get, the affection remains. Many animals, even if ill-treated, do not lose their love which means remarkable psychic development in the vital.

SRI AUROBINDO

The emotional being of animals is often much more psychic

than that of men who can be very insensitive. There were recently pictures of the tame tigress kept by a family and afterwards given by them to a Zoo. The look of sorrow on the face of the tigress in her cage at once gentle and tragically poignant is so intense as to be heart-breaking.

SRI AUROBINDO

In children the psychic is always in the front, isn't it?

Not always. The psychic is more "in front" than later when they grow up and the mind develops, but it can't be said that in all children the psychic may be felt. And one cannot judge from what we have here, for the condition of admission I make when children are brought to me is this: if I see the psychic on the surface I take them, but if they are already veiled by all sorts of deformed activities, I don't take them. So, those whom we have here are an exception. It is the cream. It is a choice.

But why are there greedy children?

Oh, good heavens! Greedy, that's not a crime! There are greedy children. Perhaps they have a bad digestion and so always want to eat. They don't gain by what they eat. The whole outer being is full of difficulties of all kinds, in everybody — in children also. You could ask me with much more justification: "Why are there such cruel children?" That indeed is one of the most dreadful things.... But it is due to unconsciousness. It is because they are not even aware that they are making others suffer. And usually, if care is taken to make them understand — for instance, through experience — then they understand. Children who ill-treat animals (there are many of these) — well, that is because they don't even know that animals feel as they do. When they are made to understand that when they pinch animals or pull their hair or beat them it gives them pain, and if necessary when they are shown on their own bodies how it hurts, they don't do it any more! There are some who are particularly wicked. These are under a perfidious influence. And at times this shows itself from their very infancy and they are like that all through their life, unless they are converted, which is not easy.

There is a sort of association between the physical and the psychic and between the mental and the vital being. A mental being is very often a very vital being. A psychic being is very often a physical being. Children — just because this psychic consciousness is in front in them — live also altogether in their body. But as soon as one begins to develop the mind, the taste for association also develops, with all the deformations that go with it. People who make very strict distinctions between man and woman (I don't know why, for one is as good as the other), say that man is mental and vital and woman physical and psychic. There is some truth in it. But naturally it involves all possible exceptions and complications. These are arbitrary simplifications. In fact the physical being has a simplicity and even a goodwill (which is not always very enlightened, far from it), but still a simplicity and goodwill which put it in a closer relation with the psychic than the passions of the vital or the pretensions of the mind. And it is probably because of that also that in children the psychic can feel more at ease, being less constantly jostled by mental and vital contradictions.

THE MOTHER

It is not yet realised what this soul is or that the true secret, whether with child or man, is to help him to find his deeper self, the real psychic entity within. That, if we ever give it a chance to come forward, and still more if we call it into the foreground as "the leader of the march set in our front," will itself take up most of the business of education out of our hands and develop the capacity of the psychological being towards a realisation of its potentialities of which our present mechanical view of life and man and external routine methods of dealing with them prevent us from having any experience or forming any conception. These new educational methods are on the straight way to this truer dealing. The closer touch attempted with the psychical entity behind the vital and physical mentality and an increasing reliance on its possibilities must lead to the ultimate discovery that man is inwardly a soul and a conscious power of the Divine and that the evocation of this real man within is the right object of education and indeed of all human life if it would find and live according to the hidden Truth and deepest law of its own being.

SRI AUROBINDO

The psychic being is formed by the inner Truth and organised around it.

THE MOTHER

Does the psychic being identify itself with the inner Truth?

It organises itself around it and enters into contact with it. The psychic is moved by the Truth. The Truth is something eternally self-existent and dependent on nothing in time or space, whereas the psychic being is a being that grows, takes form, progresses, individualises itself more and more. In this way it becomes more and more capable of manifesting this Truth, the eternal Truth that is one and permanent. The psychic being is a progressive being, which means that the relation between the psychic being and the Truth is a progressive one. It is not possible to become aware of one's psychic being without becoming aware at the same time of the inner Truth. All those who have had this experience — not a mental experience but an integral experience of contact with the psychic being, not a contact with the idea they have constructed of it, but a truly concrete contact — all say the same thing: from the very minute this contact takes place, one is absolutely conscious of the eternal Truth within oneself and one sees that it is the purpose of life and the guide of the world.

THE MOTHER

Can one be in contact with the eternal Truth without having any contact with one's psychic being?

Some beings in the universe may have this direct contact with the eternal Truth without any contact with the psychic being, because they don't have any psychic being. But in man there is always a psychic being, and it is always through it that he comes into contact with the eternal Truth. And this contact with the psychic being is usually disclosed to him in the same way, for it carries with it its own grace, its own splendour and beatitude. The psychic being is characteristic of man, and if one goes to the bottom of the matter, perhaps this is what gives man his superiority.

THE MOTHER

Can a child become conscious of this inner truth like an adult?

For a child this is very clear, for it is a perception without any complications of word or thought — there is that which puts him at ease and that which makes him uneasy (it is not necessarily joy or sorrow which come only when the thing is very intense). And all this is much clearer in the child than in an adult, for the latter has always a mind which works and clouds his perception of the truth.

To give a child theories is absolutely useless, for as soon as his mind awakes he will find a thousand reasons for contradicting your theories, and he will be right.

This little true thing in the child is the divine Presence in the psychic — it is also there in plants and animals. In plants it is not conscious, in animals it begins to be conscious, and in children it is very conscious. I have known children who were much more conscious of their psychic being at the age of five than at fourteen, and at fourteen than at twenty-five; and above all, from the moment they go to school where they undergo that kind of intensive mental training which draws their attention to the intellectual part of their being, they lose almost always and almost completely this contact with their psychic being.

If only you were an experienced observer, if you could tell what goes on in a person, simply by looking into his eyes!... it is said the eyes are the mirror of the soul; that is a popular way of speaking but if the eyes do not express to you the psychic, it is because it is very far behind, veiled by many things. Look carefully, then, into the eyes of little children, and you will see a kind of light — some describe it as frank — but so true, so true, which looks at the world with wonder. Well, this sense of wonder, it is the wonder of the psychic which sees the truth but does not understand much about the world, for it is too far from it. Children have this but as they learn more, become more intelligent, more educated, this is effaced, and you see all sorts of things in their eyes: thoughts, desires, passions, wickedness — but this kind of little flame, so pure, is no longer there. And you may be sure it is the mind that has got in there, and the psychic has gone very far behind.

Even a child who does not have a sufficiently developed brain to understand, if you simply pass on to him a vibration of protection or affection or solicitude or consolation, you will see that he responds. But if you take a boy of fourteen, for example, who is at school, who has ordinary parents and has been ill-treated, his mind is very much in the forefront; there is something hard in him, the psychic being has gone behind. Such boys do not respond to the vibration. One would say they are made of wood or plaster.

THE MOTHER

If the inner truth, the divine presence in the psychic is so conscious in the child, it could no longer be said that a child is a little animal, could it?

Why not? In animals there is sometimes a very intense psychic truth. Naturally, I believe that the psychic being is a little more formed, a little more conscious in a child than in an animal. But I have experimented with animals, just to know; well, I assure you that in human beings I have rarely come across some of the virtues which I have seen in animals, very simple, unpretentious virtues. As in cats, for example: I have studied cats a lot; if one knows them well they are marvellous creatures. I have known mother-cats which have sacrificed themselves entirely for their babies — people speak of maternal love with such admiration, as though it were purely a human privilege, but I have seen this love manifested by mother-cats to a degree far surpassing ordinary humanity. I have seen a mother-cat which would never touch her food until her babies had taken all they needed. I have seen another cat which stayed eight days beside her kittens, without satisfying any of her needs because she was afraid to leave them alone; and a cat which repeated more than fifty times the same movement to teach her young one how to jump from a wall on to a window, and I may add, with a care, an intelligence, a skill which many uneducated women do not have. And why is it thus? — because there was no mental intervention. It was altogether spontaneous instinct. But what is instinct? — it is the presence of the Divine in the genus of the species, and that, that is the psychic of animals; a collective, not an individual psychic.

I have seen in animals all the reactions, emotional, affective, sentimental, all the feelings of which men are so proud. The only difference is that animals cannot speak of them and write about them, so we consider them inferior beings because they cannot flood us with books on what they have felt.

THE MOTHER

Mother, here Sri Aurobindo speaks of "the psychic behind supporting all". What does this mean?

Well, yes, the psychic is behind the whole organisation, this triple organisation of human life and consciousness, the psychic is behind and supports it by its consciousness which is an immortal one. It is because of the psychic that we have so clear a sense of continuity. Otherwise if you compare what you now are with what you were when you were three, obviously you couldn't recognise yourself in any way, either physically or vitally or mentally. There is no resemblance of any kind. But behind there is the psychic which supports the development, the growth of the being and gives this continuity of consciousness, makes one feel that he is the same being even while being absolutely different, absolutely different. If later one observes himself sufficiently, he can see that the things he understood and could do at that time are things which seem to him absolutely inconceivable now, and that he could never do a similar thing because he is no longer that person at all. And yet, because within there was the psychic consciousness which is immortal, one has the feeling that it is always the same being which was there and continues to be there and will continue to be there with more or less progressive and more or less conscious changes.

THE MOTHER

There is another [remedy for fear of dying], a little more difficult, but better, I believe. It lies in telling oneself: "This body is not I", and in trying to find in oneself the part which is truly one's self, until one has found one's psychic being. And when one has found one's psychic being — immediately, you understand — one has the sense of immortality. And one knows that what goes out or what comes in is just a matter of convenience: "I am not going to weep over a pair of shoes I put aside when it is full of holes! When my pair of shoes is worn out I cast it aside, and I do not weep." Well, the psychic being has taken this body because it needed to use it for its work, but when the time comes to leave the body, that is to say, when one must leave it because it is no longer of any use for some reason or other, one leaves the body and has no fear. It is quite a natural gesture — and it is done without the least regret, that's all.

And the moment you are in your psychic being, you have that feeling, spontaneously, effortlessly. You soar above the physical life and have the sense of immortality. As for me, I consider this the best remedy. The other is an intellectual, common-sense, rational remedy. This is a deep experience and you can always get it back as soon as you recover the contact with your psychic being. This is a truly interesting phenomenon, for it is automatic. The moment you are in contact with your psychic being, you have the feeling of immortality, of having always been and being always, eternally.

And then what comes and goes — these are life's accidents, they have no importance.

THE MOTHER

Sweet Mother, can the psychic express itself without the mind, the vital and the physical?

It expresses itself constantly without them. Only, in order that the ordinary human being may perceive it, it has to express itself through them, because the ordinary human being is not in direct contact with the psychic. If it was in direct contact with the psychic it would be psychic in its manifestation — and all would be truly well. But as it is not in contact with the psychic it doesn't even know what it is, it wonders all bewildered what kind of a being it can be; so to reach this ordinary human consciousness it must use ordinary means, that is, go through the mind, the vital and the physical.

One of them may be skipped but surely not the last, otherwise one is no longer conscious of anything at all.

THE MOTHER

The reign of reason should not end until the coming of the psychic law which manifests the Divine Will.

THE MOTHER

Every soul is not evolved and active; nor is every soul turned directly to the Divine before practising yoga. For a long time it seeks the Divine through men and things much more than directly.

SRI AUROBINDO

More Lights on the Psychic Being

The source of sincerity, of will, of perseverance is in the psychic being, but this translates itself differently in different people. Generally it is in the higher part of the mind that this begins to take shape, but for it to be effective at least one part of the vital must respond, because the intensity of your will comes from there, the realising power of the will comes from its contact with the vital. If there were only refractory elements in the vital, you would not be able to do anything at all. But there is always something, somewhere, which is willing — it is perhaps something insignificant, but there is always something which is willing. It is enough to have had once one minute of aspiration and a will even if it be very fugitive, to become conscious of the Divine, to realise the Divine, for it to flash like lightning through the whole being — there are even cells of the body which respond. This is not visible all at once, but there is a response everywhere. And it is by slowly, carefully putting together all these parts which have responded, though it be but once, that one can build up something which will be coherent and organised, and which will permit one's action to continue with will, sincerity and perseverance.

Even a fleeting idea in a child, at a certain moment in its childhood when the psychic being is most in front, if it succeeds in penetrating through the outer consciousness and giving the child just an impression of something beautiful which must be realised, it creates a little nucleus and upon this you build your action. There is a vast mass of humanity to whom one would never say, "You must realise the Divine" or "Do yoga to find the Divine." If you observe well you will see that it is a tiny minority to whom this can be said. It means that this minority of beings is "prepared" to do yoga, it is that. It is that there has been a beginning of realisation — a beginning is enough. With others it is perhaps an old thing, an awakening which may come from past lives. But we are speaking of those who are less ready; they are those who have had at a certain moment a flash which has passed through their whole being and created a response, but that suffices. This does not happen to many people. Those ready to do yoga are not many if you compare them with the unconscious human mass. But one thing is certain, the fact that you are all here proves that at the least you have had that — there are those who are very far on the path (sometimes they have no idea about it), but at the least all of you have had that, that kind of spontaneous integral contact which is like an electric shock, a lightning-flash which goes through you and wakes you up to something: there is something to be realised. It is possible that the experience is not translated into words, only into a flame. That is enough. And it is around this nucleus that one organises oneself, slowly, slowly, progressively. And once it is there it never disappears. It is only if you have made a pact with the adverse forces and make a considerable effort to break the contact and not notice its existence, that you may believe it has disappeared. And yet a single flash suffices for it to come back.

If you have had this just once, you may tell yourself that in this life or another you are sure to realise.

THE MOTHER

The complete unification of the whole being around the psychic centre is the essential condition to realise a perfect sincerity.

THE MOTHER

Compassion and gratitude are essentially psychic virtues. They appear in the consciousness only when the psychic being takes part in active life.

The vital and the physical experience them as weaknesses, for they curb the free expression of their impulses, which are based on the power of strength.

As always, the mind, when insufficiently educated, is the accomplice of the vital being and the slave of the physical nature, whose laws, so overpowering in their half-conscious mechanism, it does not fully understand. When the mind awakens to the awareness of the first psychic movements, it distorts them in its ignorance and changes compassion into pity or at best into charity, and gratitude into the wish to repay, followed, little by little, by the capacity to recognise and admire.

It is only when the psychic consciousness is all-powerful in the being that compassion for all that needs help, in whatever domain, and gratitude for all that manifests the divine presence and grace, in whatever form, are expressed in all their original and luminous purity, without mixing compassion with any trace of condescension or gratitude with any sense of inferiority.

THE MOTHER

The ease and peace are felt very deep and far within because they are in the psychic and the psychic is very deep within us, covered over by the mind and vital. When you meditate you open to the psychic, become aware of your psychic consciousness deep within and feel these things. In order that these ease and peace and happiness may become strong and stable and felt in all the being and in the body, you have to go still deeper within and bring out the full force of the psychic into the physical. This can most easily be done by regular concentration and meditation with the aspiration for this true consciousness. It can be done by work also, by dedication, by doing the work for the Divine only without thought of self and keeping the idea of consecration to the Mother always in the heart. But this is not easy to do perfectly.

SRI AUROBINDO

Sweet Mother, what does "psychic poise" mean?

Psychic poise means the poise of the being which comes from the fact that the psychic, which governs the movements of the being, is the master of all the movements of the consciousness. The psychic is always well poised. So when it is active and governs the being, it inevitably brings a balance.

THE MOTHER

Then why is it said: "The psychic poise is necessary"?

Yes. This means that the help of the psychic poise is necessary. It is not that the psychic being has to become balanced: it is that one must be under the influence of the psychic poise. The psychic is always balanced. But the being is not always under the influence of the psychic which brings the balance.

More Lights on the Psychic Being

The influence of the psychic gives the balance.

THE MOTHER

There are many different reasons which make one feel at times more alive, more full of force and joy.... Usually, in ordinary life, there are people who, due to their very constitution, the way they are made, are in a certain harmony with Nature, as though they breathed with the same rhythm, and these people are usually always joyful, happy; they succeed in all they do, they avoid many troubles and catastrophes, indeed they are in harmony with the rhythm of life and Nature. And, moreover, there are days when one is in contact with the divine Consciousness which is at work, with Grace, and then everything is tinged, coloured with this Presence, and things which usually seem to you dull and uninteresting become charming, pleasant, attractive, instructive — everything lives and vibrates, and is full of promise and force. So, when one opens to that, one feels stronger, freer, happier, full of energy, and *everything* has a meaning. One understands why things are as they are and one participates in the general movement.

There are other times when, for some reason or other, one is clouded or closed or down in a hole, and so one no longer feels anything and all things lose their taste, their interest, their value; one goes about like a walking block of wood.

Now, if one is able to consciously unite with one's psychic being, one can *always* be in this state of receptivity, inner joy, energy, progress, communion with the divine Presence. And when one is in communion with That, one sees it everywhere, in everything, and all things take on their true meaning.

On what does that depend?... On an inner rhythm. Perhaps a grace. In any case on a receptivity to something that is beyond you.

THE MOTHER

Indeed, the expression of a true psychic life in the being is peace, a joyful serenity.

Any suffering is therefore a precious indication to us of our weak point, of the point which demands a greater spiritual effort from us.

THE MOTHER

True happiness does not depend on the external circumstances of life. One can obtain true happiness and keep it constantly only by discovering one's psychic being and uniting with it.

THE MOTHER

I think the more psychic one is, usually, the more difficulties he has. Only, one is armed to face the difficulties. But the more psychic one is, the more is he in contradiction with the present state of the world. So when one is in opposition with something, the result is difficulties. And I have noticed that most often those who have many difficulties are those who are in a more or less close contact with their psychic being. If you want to speak about outer circumstances — I am not speaking of the character, that's quite different, but of outer circumstances — the people who have to struggle most and would have most reason to suffer are those who have a very

More Lights on the Psychic Being

developed psychic being.

First, the development of the psychic being has a double result which is concomitant. That is, with the development of the psychic being, the sensitivity of the being grows. And with the growth of sensitivity there is also the growth of the capacity for suffering; but there is the counterpart, that is, to the extent to which one is in relation with the psychic being, one faces the circumstances of life in an altogether different way and with a kind of inner freedom which makes one capable of withdrawing from a circumstance and not feeling the shock in the ordinary way. You can face the difficulty or outer things with calm, peace, and a sufficient inner knowledge not to be troubled. So, on one side you are more sensitive and on the other you have more strength to deal with the sensitivity.

THE MOTHER

It is not the psychic being that suffers for personal reasons, it is the mind, the vital and the ordinary consciousness of ignorant man. This is because the contact between the outer consciousness and the psychic consciousness is not well established. He in whom the contact has been well established is always happy.

The psychic being works with perseverance and ardour for the union to be made an accomplished fact, but it never complains and knows how to wait for the hour of realisation to come.

THE MOTHER

The pure psychic being is of the essence of Ananda, it comes from the delight-soul in the universe; but the superficial heart of emotion is overborne by the conflicting appearances of the world and suffers many reactions of grief, fear, depression, passion, shortlived and partial joy.

SRI AUROBINDO

You can multiply your possibilities, enlarge and increase them; you can suddenly bring up something you did not think you had…. When one discovers one's psychic being within, at the same time there develop and manifest, quite unexpectedly, things one could not do at all before and which one didn't think were in one's nature. Of this too I have had numerous examples….

I used to know a young girl who was born in a very ordinary environment, who had not received much education and wrote rather clumsy French, who had not developed her imagination and had absolutely no literary sense: that seemed to be among the possibilities she did not have. Well, when she had the inner experience of contact with her psychic being, and as long as the contact was living and very present, she wrote admirable things. When she fell back from that state into an ordinary one, she could not even put two sentences together correctly! And I saw examples of both kinds of her writing.

There is a genius within everyone of us — we don't know it. We must find the way to make it come out — but it is there sleeping, it asks for nothing better than to manifest; we must open the door to it.

THE MOTHER

More Lights on the Psychic Being

I have also been asked if the psychic being or psychic consciousness is the medium through which the inspiration is perceived.

Generally, yes. The first contact you have with higher regions is a psychic one. Certainly, before an inner psychic opening is achieved, it is difficult to have these inspirations. It can happen as an exception and under exceptional conditions as a grace, but the true contact comes through the psychic; because the psychic consciousness is certainly the medium with the greatest affinity with the divine Truth.

Later, when one has emerged from the mental consciousness into a higher consciousness beyond the mind, beyond even the higher mind, and when one opens oneself to the Overmind regions, and through the Overmind to the Supermind, one can receive inspirations directly. And naturally at that point they become more frequent, richer, if one may say so, more complete. There comes a time when inspiration can be obtained at will, but this obviously demands considerable inner development.

THE MOTHER

Each one of you should be able to get into touch with your own psychic being, it is not an inaccessible thing. Your psychic being is there precisely to put you in contact with the divine forces. And if you are in contact with your psychic being, you begin to feel, to have a kind of perception of what divine Love can be. As I have just said, it is not enough that one morning you wake up saying, "Oh! I would like to be in contact with divine Love", it is not like that. If, through a sustained effort, a deep concentration, a great forgetfulness of self, you succeed in coming into touch with your psychic being, you will never dream of thinking, "Oh! I would like to be in contact with divine Love" — you are in a state in which everything appears to you to be this divine Love and nothing else. And yet it is only a covering, but a covering of a beautiful texture.

So, divine Love need not be sought and known apart from the psychic being?

No, find your psychic being and you will understand what divine Love is. Do not try to come into direct contact with divine Love because this will yet again be a vital desire pushing you; you will perhaps not be aware of it, but it will be a vital desire.

You must make an effort to come into touch with your psychic being, to become aware and free in the consciousness of your psychic being, and then, quite naturally, spontaneously, you will know what divine Love is.

THE MOTHER

On the physical plane the Divine expresses himself through beauty, on the mental plane through knowledge, on the vital plane through power and on the psychic plane through love.

When we rise high enough, we discover that these four aspects unite with each other in a single consciousness, full of love, luminous, powerful, beautiful, containing all, pervading all.

It is only to satisfy the universal play that this consciousness divides itself into several lines or aspects of manifestation.

THE MOTHER

The deeper the emotion, the more intense the Bhakti, the greater is the force for realisation and transformation. It is oftenest through intensity of emotion that the psychic being awakes and there is an opening of the inner doors to the Divine.

SRI AUROBINDO

Emotion is a good element in yoga; but emotional desire becomes easily a cause of perturbation and an obstacle.

Turn your emotions towards the Divine, aspire for their purification; they will then become a help on the way and no longer a cause of suffering.

Not to kill emotion, but to turn it towards the Divine is the right way of the yoga.

But it must become pure, founded upon spiritual peace and joy, capable of being transmuted into Ananda. Equality and calm in the mind and vital parts, an intense psychic emotion in the heart can perfectly go together.

Awake by your aspiration the psychic fire in the heart that burns steadily towards the Divine — that is the one way to liberate and fulfil the emotional nature.

SRI AUROBINDO

It is only the ordinary vital emotions which waste the energy and disturb the concentration and peace that have to be discouraged. Emotion itself is not a bad thing; it is a necessary part of the nature, and psychic emotion is one of the most powerful helps to the sadhana. Psychic emotion, bringing tears of love for the Divine or tears of Ananda, ought not to be suppressed: it is only a vital mixture that brings disturbance in the sadhana.

SRI AUROBINDO

The emotional [devotion] is more outward than the psychic — it tends towards outward expression. The psychic is inwards and gives the direction to the whole inner and outer life. The emotional can be intense, but is neither so sure in its basis nor powerful enough to change the whole direction of the life.

SRI AUROBINDO

How many times have we repeated this: all that comes from the mind is wholly relative. The more the mind is educated and has applied itself to various disciplines, the more it becomes capable of proving that what it puts forward or what it says is true. One can prove the truth of anything by reasoning, but that does not make it true. It remains an opinion, a prejudice, a knowledge based on appearances which are themselves more than dubious.

So there seems to be only one way out and that is to go in search of one's soul and to find it. It is there, it does not make a point of hiding itself, it does not play with you just to make things difficult; on the contrary, it makes great efforts to help you find it and to make itself heard. Only, between your soul and your active consciousness there are two characters who are in the habit of making a lot of noise, the mind

More Lights on the Psychic Being

and the vital. And because they make a lot of noise, while the soul does not, or, rather, makes as little as possible, their noise prevents you from hearing the voice of the soul.

When you want to know what your soul knows, you have to make an inner effort, to be very attentive; and indeed, if you are attentive, behind the outer noise of the mind and the vital, you can discern something very subtle, very quiet, very peaceful, which knows and says what it knows. But the insistence of the others is so imperious, while *that* is so quiet, that you are very easily misled into listening to the one that makes the most noise; most often you become aware only afterwards that the other one was right. It does not impose itself, it does not compel you to listen, for it is without violence.

When you hesitate, when you wonder what to do in this or that circumstance, there come the desire, the preference both mental and vital, that press, insist, affirm and impose themselves, and, with the best reasons in the world, build up a whole case for themselves. And if you are not on the alert, if you don't have a firm discipline, if you don't have the habit of control, they finally convince you that they are right. And as I was saying a little while ago, they make so much noise that you do not even hear the tiny voice or the tiny, very quiet indication of the soul which says, "Don't do it."

This "Don't do it" comes often, but you discard it as something which has no power and follow your impulsive destiny. But if you are truly sincere in your will to find and live the truth, then you learn to listen better and better, you learn to discriminate more and more, and even if it costs you an effort, even if it causes you pain, you learn to obey. And even if you have obeyed only once, it is a powerful help, a considerable progress on the path towards the discrimination between what is and what is not the soul. With this discrimination and the necessary sincerity you are sure to reach the goal.

But you must not be in a hurry, you must not be impatient, you must be very persevering. You do the wrong thing ten times for every time that you do the right thing. But when you do the wrong thing you must not give up everything in despair, but tell yourself that the Grace will never abandon you and that next time it will be better.

So, in conclusion, we shall say that in order to know things as they are you must first unite with your soul and to unite with your soul you must want it with persistence and perseverance.

Only the degree of concentration on the goal can shorten the way.

THE MOTHER

Sweet Mother, with the human mind is it possible to recognise another person's soul?

Things are not so clear-cut and separate as they are in speaking; that is just why it is quite difficult to see very distinctly and clearly in oneself the different parts of the being, unless one has had a very long training and a long discipline of study and observation. There are no watertight compartments between the soul and the mind, the vital and even the physical. There is an infiltration of the soul into the mind. In some people it is even quite considerable, it is perceptible. So, the part of the mind which has a kind of sensibility, of subtle

More Lights on the Psychic Being

contact with the psychic being, is capable of feeling the presence of the soul in others.

Those who have the ability to enter to a certain extent into the consciousness of others to the point of being able to see or feel directly their thought, their mental activity, who can enter the mental atmosphere of others without needing to use words to make themselves understood, can easily differentiate between someone whose soul is active and someone whose soul is asleep. The activity of the soul gives a special colouring to the mental activity — it is lighter, more comprehensive and luminous — so that can be felt. For instance, by looking into someone's eyes you can say with some certainty that this person has a living soul or that you don't see his soul in his eyes. Many people can feel — "many", I mean among evolved people — can say that. But naturally, to know exactly how far somebody's soul is awake and active, how far it rules the being, is the master, one must have the psychic consciousness oneself, for that alone can judge definitively. But it is not altogether impossible to have that sort of inner vibration which makes you say, "Oh! This person has a soul."

Now, obviously, most often what people — unless they are initiated — call "soul" is the vital activity. If someone has a strong, active, obstinate vital which rules the body's activities, which has a very living or intense contact with people and things and events, if he has a marked taste for art, for all expressions of beauty, we are generally tempted to say and believe, "Oh! he has a living soul"; but it is not his soul, it is his vital being which is alive and dominates the activities of the body. That is the first difference between someone who is beginning to be developed and those who are still in the inertia and *tamas* of the purely material life. This gives, first to the appearance and also to the activity, a kind of vibration, of intensity of vibration, which often creates the impression that this person has a living soul; but it is not that, it is his vital which is developed, which has a special capacity, is stronger than the physical inertia and gives an intensity of vibration and life and action that those whose vital being is not developed do not possess. This confusion between the vital activity and the soul is a very frequent one.... The vital vibration is much more easily perceptible to the human consciousness than the vibration of the soul.

To perceive the soul in someone, as a rule the mind must be very quiet — very quiet, for when it is active, *its* vibrations are seen, not the vibration of the soul.

And then, when you look at someone who is conscious of his soul, and lives in his soul, if you look like this, the impression you have is of descending, of entering deep, deep, deep into the person, far, far, far, far within; while usually when you look into someone's eyes, you very soon come to a surface which vibrates and answers your look, but you don't have that feeling of going down, down, down, down, going deep as into a hole and very far, very, very, very far within, so you have... a small, very quiet response. Otherwise, usually you enter — there are eyes you cannot enter, they are closed like a door; but still there are eyes which are open — you enter and then, quite close behind, you come to something vibrating there, like this, shining at times, vibrating. And then, that's it; if you make a mistake, you say, "Oh! he has a living soul" — it is not that, it is his vital.

More Lights on the Psychic Being

In order to find the soul you must go in this way (*gesture of going deep within*), like this, draw back from the surface, withdraw deep within and enter, enter, enter, go down, down, down into a very deep hole, silent, immobile, and there, there's a kind of... something warm, quiet, rich in substance and very still, and very full, like a sweetness — that is the soul.

And if one is insistent and is conscious oneself, then there comes a kind of plenitude which gives the feeling of something complete that contains unfathomable depths in which, should one enter, one feels that many secrets would be revealed... like the reflection in very peaceful waters of something that is eternal. And one no longer feels limited by time.

One has the feeling of having always been and of being for eternity.

That is when one has touched the core of the soul.

And if the contact has been conscious and complete enough, it liberates you from the bondage of outer form; you no longer feel that you live only because you have a body. That is usually the ordinary sensation of the being, to be so tied to this outer form that when one thinks of "myself" one thinks of the body. That is the usual thing. The personal reality is the body's reality. It is only when one has made an effort for inner development and tried to find something that is a little more stable in one's being, that one can begin to feel that this "something" which is permanently conscious throughout all ages and all change, this something must be "myself". But that already requires a study that is rather deep. Otherwise if you think "I am going to do this", "I need that", it is always your body, a small kind of will which is a mixture of sensations, of more or less confused sentimental reactions, and still more confused thoughts which form a mixture and are animated by an impulse, an attraction, a desire, some sort of a will; and all that momentarily becomes "myself" — but not directly, for one does not conceive this "myself" as independent of the head, the trunk, the arms and legs and all that moves — it is very closely linked.

It is only after having thought much, seen much, studied much, observed much that you begin to realise that the one is more or less independent of the other and that the will behind can make it either act or not act, and you begin not to be completely identified with the movement, the action, the realisation — that something is floating. But you have to observe much to see that.

And then you must observe much more still to see that this, the second thing that is there, this kind of active conscious will, is set in motion by "something else" which watches, judges, decides and tries to found its decisions on knowledge — that happens even much later. And so, when you begin to see this "something else", you begin to see that it has the power to set in motion the second thing, which is an active will; and not only that, but that it has a very direct and very important action on the reactions, the feelings, the sensations, and that finally it can have control over all the movements of the being — this part which watches, observes, judges and decides.

That is the beginning of control.

When one becomes conscious of that, one has seized the thread, and when one speaks of control, one can know, "Ah! yes, this is what has the power of control."

This is how one learns to look at oneself.

THE MOTHER

When humanity was first created, the ego was the unifying element. It was around the ego that the different states of being were grouped; but now that the birth of superhumanity is being prepared, the ego has to disappear and give way to the psychic being, which has slowly been formed by divine intervention in order to manifest the Divine in the human being.

It is under the psychic influence that the Divine manifests in man and thus prepares the coming of superhumanity.

The psychic is immortal and it is through the psychic that immortality can be manifested on earth.

So the important thing now is to find one's psychic, unite with it and allow it to replace the ego, which will be compelled either to get converted or disappear.

THE MOTHER

GLOSSARY

(Most of the explanations of terms given below have been derived from Sri Aurobindo's writings.)

ādhāra (Adhar)
: vehicle (vessel, support); that in which the consciousness is now contained, mind-life-body.

Adverse forces
: *See* Hostile forces

agni (Agni)
: the godhead of fire.

agni pāvaka
: the purifying fire; the psychic fire.

ānanda (Ananda)
: bliss, delight, beatitude, spiritual ecstasy; the essential principle of delight; a self-delight which is the very nature of the transcendent and infinite existence.

annamaya puruṣa (Annamaya Purusha)
: soul in body; physical conscious being; material being.

aparā prakṛti
: the lower Nature, the external objective and superficial subjective apparent nature which manifests all minds, lives and bodies.

asura (Asura)
: the strong or mighty one, Titan; a hostile being.

Asuric
: pertaining to an *asura* or Titan or hostile being.

ātman (Atman)
: Self: Spirit; the original and essential nature of our exist-

ence; the true and highest Self.

avatāra (Avatar)
Incarnation; the descent into form; the revelation of the godhead in humanity; the divine manifest in a human appearance.

avidyā (Avidya)
the Ignorance; the consciousness of Multiplicity; the relative and multiple consciousness.

bhakta (Bhakta)
a lover and devotee of the Divine.

bhakti (Bhakti)
love for the Divine, devotion to the Divine.

bindu (Bindu)
dot, point.

brahman (Brahman)
the Reality; the eternal; the Absolute; the Spirit; the Supreme being; the one besides whom there is nothing else existent.

caitya puruṣa (Chaitya Purusha)
psychic Person; the psychic being.

Chitta see *citta*

citta (Chitta)
basic consciousness; mind-stuff, the general stuff of mental consciousness.

Consciousness
the fundamental thing in existence; it is the Energy, the motion, the Movement of consciousness that creates the universe and all that is in it.

Consciousness-Force
the Force that builds the worlds; all action, all mental, vi-

Glossary

tal, physical activities in the world are the operation of a universal Energy, a Consciousness-Force which is the power of the Cosmic Spirit working out the cosmic and individual truth of things.

Delight-soul

the all-blissful being or all-enjoying and all-productive soul; and infinite "I Am" of bliss.

Desire-soul

the surface soul in us which works in our vital cravings, our emotions, aesthetic faculty and mental seeking for power, knowledge and happiness.

devayāna

a journeying of the gods or to the gods.

dharma (Dharma)

law of being, standard of truth, rule or law of action; the collective Indian conception of the religious, social and moral rule and conduct; ethical conduct and the right law of individual and social life.

the Divine

the Supreme Truth, the Supreme Being from whom all have come and in whom all are.

Ego

a shadow and projection of the spiritual individuality; it implies an identification of the true Self with outer self of mind, life and body; the ego is therefore mental, vital and physical.

the Force

the power of being in motion; the divine Force.

Higher Mind

one of the planes of the spiritual mind, the first and lowest of them; a first plane of spiritual consciousness.

Hostile forces
> forces which try to pervert everything and are in revolt against the Divine and opposed to the Yoga.

hṛdaye guhāyām
> in the heart — the secret heart-cave.

the Ignorance
> a veil that separates the Mind, Body, and Life from their source and reality, Sachchidananda; the consciousness of being in the successions of Time, divided in its knowledge by dwelling in the divisions of Space and the relations of circumstance, self-prisoned in the multiple working of the unity; it is called ignorance because it has put behind it the Knowledge of unity and by that very fact is unable to know truly or completely either itself or the world, either the transcendent or the universal reality.

the Inconscience (Inconscient)
> in its cosmic manifestation the Supreme, being the Infinite and not bound by any limitation, manifests in itself, in its consciousness of innumerable possibilities, something that seems to be the opposite of itself, something in which there can be Darkness, Inconscience, Inertia, Insensibility, Disharmony and Disintegration; it is the Inconscient that is at the basis of the material world.

Inmost being
> *see* psychic being

Inner being
> the inner mind, inner vital, inner physical with the psychic behind as the inmost; the inner being is the true being.

Inner mental

    that which lies behind the surface mind, our ordinary mentality; it is a part of the inner being.

Inner physical

    see Inner being

Inner vital

    see Inner being

Integral Yoga

    the full yoga, Purna Yoga; a fourfold path: a Yoga of Knowledge for the mind, a Yoga of Bhakti for the heart, a Yoga of Works for the Will and a Yoga of Perfection for the whole nature; its two main elements are — first, the acceptance of the world as a manifestation of the Divine Power, not its rejection as a mistake or an illusion, and, secondly, the character of this manifestation as a spiritual evolution with yoga as a means for the transformation of mind, life and body into instruments of a spiritual and supramental perfection.

Intermediate zone

    a confused condition or passage in which one is getting out of the personal consciousness and opening into the Cosmic (cosmic Mind, cosmic vital, cosmic physical, something perhaps of the cosmic Higher Mind) without having yet transcended the human mind levels; one is not in possession of or direct contact with the divine Truth *on its own levels*, but one can receive something from them, even from the overmind, indirectly; only, as one is still immersed in the cosmic ignorance, all that comes from above can be mixed, perverted, taken hold of for their purposes by lower, even by hostile Powers.

īśvara-śakti (Ishwara-Shakti)
: the dual principle of the lord (*īśvara*) and his executive Power (*śakti*).

jīvātman (Jivatman)
: the individual self; central being; the *ātman*, spirit or eternal self of the living being; the multiple Divine manifested here as the individualised self or spirit of the created being.

karma (Karma)
: action; work; the principle of cause and effect in human life; accumulated seeds of past action.

the Knowledge
: consciousness of the Truth; unifying consciousness of the One Reality.

kṣara puruṣa (Kshara Purusha)
: the soul in nature; the spirit in the mutability of cosmic phenomenon and becoming.

the Life
: *see* Life-force

Life-force
: the pure vital energy or life-energy, called Prana in Sanskrit.

manomaya puruṣa (Manomaya Purusha)
: mental Person; mental being

the Mental
: *see* Mind

Mental sheath
: one of the three sheaths of consciousness in us: the three are the material, *annakoṣa*, in which the physical contact and image are received and formed; the vital or nervous,

prāṇakoṣa, in which there is a nervous contact and formation, and, the mental, *manaḥkoṣa*, in which there is mental contact and imaging.

Mental world
a world of mental existence in which neither life, nor matter, but mind is the first determinant.

Mind
in its ordinary use, the word covers indiscriminately the whole consciousness; for man is a mental being and mentalises everything; but in the language of yoga the words "mind" and "mental" are used to connote specially the part of the nature which has to do with cognition and intelligence, with ideas, with mental or thought perception, the reactions of thought to things, with the truly mental movements and formations, mental vision and will, etc., that are part of his intelligence.

mokṣa (Moksha)
release, liberation; spiritual liberation

mukti (Mukti)
liberation

nirvāna (Nirvana)
extinction of ego, desire and egoistic action and mentality.

Outer being
the surface being in us made up of our ordinary exterior mind, life, body consciousness as opposed to the inner being constituted of an inner mind, an inner life, an inner physical consciousness, which remains behind the veil.

Overhead planes
successive states, levels, planes or graded powers of being overtopping our normal mind, hidden in our own super-

Overmind
   the highest of the planes below the supramental.
pāpa (Papa)
   sin, demerit
parameśvara (Parameshwara)
   supreme Lord
parā prakṛti
   the supreme Nature; the very nature of the Divine; the infinite timeless conscious power of the self-existent being out of which all existences in the cosmos are manifested .
parā prakṛtir jīvabhūtā
   the spiritual Nature which has become the *jīva* Jivatman
Personality
   a complex composite of Nature, with many layers, and with strata within each stratum; a temporary mental, vital, physical formation which the being, the real Person, the psychic entity, puts forward on the surface.
the Physical
   outermost part of the being; everything has a physical part — there is a mental physical, a mind of the body; the emotional being has a physical part; the material is the most physical of the physical.
pitṛyāna
   the road of the Fathers, supposed to lead to inferior worlds attained by the Fathers who still belong to the evolution in the Ignorance.
prakṛti (Prakriti)
   "working out"; Nature; nature-Force.

prāṇamaya puruṣa (Pranamaya Purusha)
: soul in life; the (true) vital being.

Psyche
: the soul; the essence of the soul; the spark of the Divine which is there in all things.

the Psychic
: psychic being; (sometimes) the psychic essence.

Psychic being
: the soul; when the psychic, spark of the Divine which is present in all life and matter, begins to develop an individuality in the course of evolution, that psychic individuality is called the psychic being.

Psychic entity
: the spark of the Divine that descends into the evolution as a divine principle within it to support the evolution of the individual out of the Ignorance into the Light; it grows behind the mind, vital and physical as the psychic being.

Psychic individuality
: the individualised soul supporting from behind the heart-centre the mental, vital, physical, psychic evolution of the being in Nature; the psychic being.

Psychic personality
: *see* Soul-personality

puṇya
: good, virtue, merit.

puruṣa (Purusha)
: Person; Conscious Being, Conscious-Soul; essential being supporting the play of *prakṛti*.

puruṣa antarātman (Purusha Antaratman)
: the Conscious Being as the inner self or soul.

Rakshasic
   pertaining to a Rakshasa or a hostile being.
sādhaka (Sadhak)
   one who is engaged in the practice of *sādhanā* or yoga.
sādhanā (Sadhana)
   the practice of yoga; the practice by which perfection (*siddhi*) is attained; spiritual self-training and exercise.
samatā (Samata)
   equality, equanimity
sarva-bhūtāni
   all existences
the Self
   our self-existent Being; the conscious essential Existence, one in all.
siddhi (Siddhi)
   perfection, fulfilment, accomplishment of the aims of self-discipline by yoga.
Soul
   see the Psyche *and* Psychic Being
Soul-personality
   the psychic being or soul-form developing through evolution and passing from life to life till all is ready for the higher evolution beyond the Ignorance.
Spark-soul
   the spark of the Divine which supports the obscure mass of the outer nature and around which grows the psychic being, the formed soul or the real Man within.
śrāddha
   certain ceremonies held in honour of and for the benefit of dead relatives.

Glossary

the Subconscient
: the quite submerged part of our being in which there is no wakingly conscious and coherent thought, will or feeling or organized reaction, but which yet receives obscurely the impressions of all things and stores them up in itself and from it too all sorts of stimuli, of persistent habitual movements, crudely repeated or disguised in strange forms can surge up into dream or into the waking nature.

the Subliminal
: comprises the inner being, taken in its entirety of inner mind, inner life, inner physical with the soul or psychic entity supporting them.

Subtle body
: the sheath and subtle-physical support of the inner being.

Subtle physical
: a subtler envelope, closest to the physical and most like it, but having a freedom, plasticity, intensity, power, colour, wide and manifold play of which, as yet, we have no possibility on earth.

the Supermind
: the full Truth-Consciousness of the Divine Nature in which there is no place for the principle of division and ignorance, and which is always a full light and knowledge superior to all mental substance or mental movement; in the supermind, mental divisions and oppositions cease, the problems created by our dividing and fragmenting mind disappear and truth is seen as a luminous whole.

tamas (Tamas)
: darkness, obscurity; the mode of ignorance and inertia; the force of inconscience.

tapasyā (Tapasya)
  effort, energism, austerity of the personal will, ascetic force, askesis; concentration of the will and energy to control the mind, vital and physical and to change them or to bring down the higher consciousness or for any other yogic purpose or high purpose.

Transformation
  the state in which the higher consciousness or nature is brought down into the mind, vital and body and takes the place of the lower.

True being
  the Purusha or conscious Being, the projection of the Divine, upholding Prakriti or Nature on the various levels of the being — mental, vital, physical.

the Truth
  the ultimate spiritual Truth

Truth-Consciousness
  the consciousness of essential truth of being; it sees the Truth directly and is in possession of it spontaneously.

upaniṣad (Upanishad)
  one of a class of Hindu sacred writings, regarded as the source of the Vedanta philosophy.

the Vital
  the Life-nature made up of desires, sensations, feelings, passions, energies of action, will of desire, reactions of the desire-soul and of all the play of possessive and other related instincts, such as anger, fear, greed, lust, etc.

Vital mind
  a sort of a mediator between the vital and the mental proper; a part of the nature of the mind whose function is not to

Glossary

think and reason, to perceive, consider and find out or value things, but to plan or dream or imagine what can be done.

Vital-physical

the nervous part of the being; the life-force closely enmeshed in the reactions, desires, needs, sensations of the body.

Vital plane/world

the world of sheer vital existence, ruled by desire and the satisfaction of impulse; the desire-world.

Vital sheath

nervous body; nervous sheath

yoga (Yoga)

a methodised effort towards self-perfection by the expression of the potentialities latent in the being and union of the human individual with the universal and transcendent existence.

yogadṛṣṭi (Yogadrishti)

yogic (power of) vision

yogin (Yogi/Yogin)

one who practises *yoga*; one who is established in realisation.

REFERENCES

The passages in this book have been selected from the following volumes of Sri Aurobindo Birth Centenary Library and the Collected Works of the Mother, published by the Sri Aurobindo Ashram, Pondicherry. The one exception is the opening passage on page 3, which is from *Sri Aurobindo: Archives and Research*, Vol. 3, No. 2, pp. 202-03.

SRI AUROBINDO BIRTH CENTENARY LIBRARY

Volume	Title
9	The Future Poetry
18	The Life Divine: Book One and Book Two, Part One
19	The Life Divine: Book Two, Part Two
20	The Synthesis of Yoga: Parts One and Two
21	The Synthesis of Yoga: Parts Three and Four
22	Letters on Yoga: Part One
23	Letters on Yoga: Parts Two and Three
24	Letters on Yoga: Part Four
25	The Mother

COLLECTED WORKS OF THE MOTHER

Volume	Title
2	Words of Long Ago
3	Questions and Answers
4	Questions and Answers 1950-51
5	Questions and Answers 1953
6	Questions and Answers 1954
7	Questions and Answers 1955
8	Questions and Answers 1956
9	Questions and Answers 1957-58
10	On Thoughts and Aphorisms

12	On Education
14	Words of the Mother
15	Words of the Mother
16	Some Answers from the Mother

The references below are given in an abbreviated form. A number set in **boldface type** indicates the page number of this book on which a given passage begins. The number which follows, if prefixed by SA, indicates the volume number of Sri Aurobindo Birth Centenary Library; if prefixed by MO, it refers to the volume number of the Collected Works of the Mother. The subsequent numbers are the pages of the particular volume from which the passage has been extracted. For example, **4a**. SA24:1605 means that the first passage on page 4 of this book is taken from volume 24 of Sri Aurobindo Birth Centenary Library, page 1605.

3. A&R3:202-03. **4a**. SA24:1605. **4b**. SA22:290. **5**. SA22:288-89. **7a**. SA22:75. **7b**. SA22:386. **8a**. MO16:247. **8b**. MO16:358. **9a**. MO16:137. **9b**. SA22:293-95. **11**. SA22:284-85. **12**. SA22:438-39. **13**. SA22:265-66. **14**. SA22:278-79. **15**. SA22:267-70. **18**. SA22:282-84. **20**. SA24:1111-12. **21**. SA23:547. **22**. MO7:263-64. **24**. SA18:220-21. **26**. SA20:140-41. **28**. SA21:144-45. **30**. SA18:225-27. **32**. MO16:249-50. **33**. SA20:145-46. **34**. MO5:394. **35a**. SA24:1108. **35b**. SA22:297. **35c**. MO16:249. **36a**. MO3:63-64. **36b**. MO4:164-65. **37**. SA9:364. **38**. MO15:343-46. **41**. SA23:817-18. **42a**. SA22:301. **42b**. MO16:242. **42c**. MO5:298. **43**. MO3:152-53. **47a**. SA22:297. **47b**. MO5:395. **47c**. MO6:160-61. **49**. MO16:229. **50**. SA19:891-95. **56a**. MO16:249. **56b**. SA22:297. **56c**. SA25:220. **57**. SA9:362-63. **58**. MO5:394-95. **59a**. MO4:261. **59b**. SA23:550. **59c**. MO15:327. **60**. MO7:222-26. **64**. MO16:412. **65**. MO12:3-5. **67**. MO5:8-11. **73**. MO9:213-15. **75**. SA19:843-45. **78**. MO3:150-51. **79a**. SA18:610. **79b**. MO4:143-47. **84a**. MO10:29-30. **84a**. MO9:268-70. **87**.

MO5:359-61. **89.** MO5:205-07. **92.** MO4:149-51. **94.** MO7:374-75. **96.** MO16:223-24. **101.** SA18:630-31. **102.** SA22:114-15. **103.** MO16:397. **105a.** SA24:1096. **105b.** SA24:1105. **106.** SA23:564-65. **107a.** SA24:1095. **107b.** SA23:1054. **108a.** SA24:1095. **108b.** SA23:902-03. **108c.** SA24:1095. **109a.** SA19:900-01. **110.** SA24:1109-10. **111a.** SA24:1097. **111b.** Sa24:1098. **112a.** SA24:1098. **112b.** MO6:396. **112c.** SA23:1001. **113.** MO6:33-34. **114a.** SA24:1100. **114b.** SA24:1099. **114c.** SA23:907. **115.** SA23:517-19. **118.** SA23:725. **119a.** SA22:341-42. **119b.** SA23:594. **119c.** SA24:1109. **120a.** SA24:1109. **120b.** SA24:1101-02. **121.** SA24:1616-17. **127a.** SA22:433. **127b.** SA22:439-41. **130a.** MO4:140. **130b.** SA22:439. **130c.** SA22:458. **131a.** SA22:434. **131b.** SA22:445-46. **132.** SA19:820-21. **133.** SA22:451-52. **135a.** SA22:443. **135b.** SA22:443-44. **136.** SA22:444-45. **137.** MO7:86-87. **139.** MO4:168. **140.** MO4:183. **141.** MO5:215-17. **144.** MO5:411-12. **145.** MO8:202-04. **148.** SA22:434. **149a.** MO15:135. **149b.** MO4:147. **150a.** MO15:137. **150b.** MO5:33-35. **152.** MO15:361-64. **156.** MO5:35. **159.** MO6:27-28. **160.** MO9:339-40. **161.** MO4:228-29. **162a.** MO6:392. **162b.** SA24:1115. **163.** MO4:139-40. **164a.** SA22:375. **164b.** SA22:365. **164c.** SA22:375. **164d.** SA22:375. **165a.** SA22:375. **165b.** MO4:141. **166a.** MO4:166-67. **166b.** SA22:500. **166c.** SA22:500. **167.** MO6:4-6. **168.** SA15:28. **169a.** MO15:323. **169b.** MO15:326. **170a.** MO15:327. **170b.** MO4:26-27. **172.** MO4:27-28. **173.** MO7:221-22. **174.** MO5:316-17. **175.** MO7:42. **176a.** MO15:246. **176b.** SA22:297. **176c.** MO4:254-56. **178a.** MO15:200-01. **178b.** MO15:297. **179a.** SA23:738-39. **179b.** MO6:393. **180a.** MO6:396. **180b.** MO8:305-06. **181a.** MO2:57. **181b.** MO16:290. **182a.** MO7:21. **182b.** MO14:357. **183a.** SA21:708-09. **183b.** MO9:396-97. **184a.** MO10:5. **184b.** MO4:245-46. **185.** MO15:6. **186a.** SA23:780. **186b.** SA23:780-81. **187a.** SA23:781. **187b.** SA23:781. **187c.** MO10:24-26. **189.** MO9:308-11. **194.** MO16:432.

SELECTED BIBLIOGRAPHY

The works of Sri Aurobindo mentioned below refer to the Sri Aurobindo Birth Centenary Library; those of the Mother refer to the Collected Works of the Mother (Centenary Edition).

SRI AUROBINDO
1. *The Life Divine*, Book Two Part Two Part One (Pondicherry: Sri Aurobindo Ashram, 1970), pp. 218-30.
2. *The Life Divine*, Book Two Part Two (Pondicherry: Sri Aurobindo Ashram, 1970) pp. 889-918.
3. *The Synthesis of Yoga*, Parts One and Two (Pondicherry: Sri Aurobindo Ashram,1970), pp. 144-47.
4. *Letters on Yoga*, Part One (Pondicherry: Sri Aurobindo Ashram, 1970), pp. 265-307.
5. *Letters on Yoga*, Part Four (Pondicherry: Sri Aurobindo Ashram, 1970), pp. 1092-1125.

THE MOTHER

1. *Questions and Answers 1950-51* (Pondicherry: Sri Aurobindo Ashram, 1972), *passim*.
2. *Questions and Answers 1953* (Pondicherry: Sri Aurobindo Ashram, 1976), *passim*.
3. *Questions and Answers 1954* (Pondicherry: Sri Aurobindo Ashram, 1979), *passim*.
4. *Questions and Answers 1955* (Pondicherry: Sri Aurobindo Ashram, 1979), *passim*.
5. *Questions and Answers 1956* (Pondicherry: Sri Aurobindo Ashram, 1977), *passim*.
6. *Questions and Answers 1957-58* (Pondicherry: Sri Aurobindo Ashram, 1977), *passim*.
7. *Words of the Mother* (Pondicherry: Sri Aurobindo Ashram, 1980), Collected Works, Volume 14, pp. 351-60.
8. *Words of the Mother* (Pondicherry: Sri Aurobindo Ashram, 1980), Collected Works, Volume 15, *passim*.

INDEX

A

Adverse forces 165
agni pāvaka 59
Angels
    and psychic being 38
Animal(s)
    consciousness of 170
    emotional being of 170
    psychic in 175, 176
Aparā prakṛti 14, 15
Arya, the 21
Asuric being
    possession by 36
Atavism(s) 90, 150
Atman, the 31
    central being and 15
    psychic being and 13
    soul and 13

B

Beauty 190
Being
    unification of 67, 69-71
Buddha, the 163
Brahman, the 14
    realisation of, and change of nature 111

C

caitya puruṣa see Chaitya Purusha *under* Purusha
Catholic religion 80
Central being 14, 17, 18
    the Atman and 14
    the Jivatman and 14
    true 111
    what incarnates 135
Centres
    for concentration 117-18
Chaitya Purusha *see under* Purusha
Children
    cruelty in 171
    still-born 149
    the psychic in 171, 172-73
    who die young 149
Compassion 183
    and pity 183
Concentration
    and becoming aware within 117-118
    heart centre and 117
    object of 117-19
    three centres of 120
    two main centres 117
Conscience 33
    ordinary 33
    voice of the soul and 33
Consciousness-Force 79
Consecration 108, 110
    and conversion 108
Control
    and the soul 198

Index

Conversion 107
  and consecration 108

D

Daemon 30, 79
Death
  review of life at 138
Delight-soul 188
Desire-soul 3, 6, 21, 24, 25, 33, 32fn *see* also Soul of desire *under* Soul
Detachment 119
Devayāna 130
Dharma, the 163
Difficulties
  psychic being and 186
Divine Force *see* Force, the
Divine Presence 185
Divine, the 190
  bringing, into Matter 135
  central being and 14, 15
  collective way of approaching 98
  instinct and 177
  Jivatman, portion of 20
  personal relation with 122
  realisation of 104
  psychic and 4, 5, 14, 16
  seeking, through men and things 180
  soul and 3, 6, 15, 19, 51
  veiled in Nature 11
  ways of approaching 104
  what determines one's approach to 98
  will to realise, and the psychic 181-82
Divine Will
  psychic law manifests 180

E

Education
  right object of 173
Ego
  and psychic being 199
Elizabeth I 96
Emotion(s)
  and the psychic 39-40, 191
  and yoga 191
  psychic and vital 39-41
Europeans 22
Evolution 75-80
  change of consciousness and 76
  physical 75
  the psychic and 75-90
  rebirth and 79
Experience(s)
  and change of nature 111
  psychic and psychological 7
Eyes
  mirror of soul 176

F

Faith 44
Fear
  of dying, remedy for 179-80
Flower

and psychic presence 170
Force, the 120, 125

G

Good
  and ill 139
Grace 61, 185, 194
Gratitude 183

H

Happiness
  and circumstances 186
Harmony 185
Heart centre 168
Homogeneity
  of being 69-72
Hostile forces
  and the psychic being 114
Hridaya 14

I

Identification
  with the psychic presence 68
Individualisation
  and progress 95
Inmost being
  action of 34
  character of 34
  coming forward of 34
  see also Psychic being
Inner being, the 18
  and the psychic being 10

Inspiration 189
Instinct
  psychic in animals 177
Intermediate Zone
  and the psychic 109
Intuition 27

J

Jivatman, the (Jivatma, Jiva)
  14, 15, 16, 18, 19, 20
  and the psychic being 13, 14

K

Knowledge 190
  of mind, an opinion 192
  of self, three steps of 103
Kshara Purusha *see under*
  Purusha

L

Life (Life-force), the 29, 31
  and the soul 29
  subliminal 30
Love 25, 189, 190
  intellectual, of God 22
  psychic love 40

M

Man
  and woman, distinctions between 172

Manomaya Purusha *see under* Purusha
Memory of past lives 137, 151-59
  in children 152
  nature of psychic memory 151, 159
  of animal lives 158
  of the vital being 153
Mental sheath *see* Sheaths
Mind
  and perception of truth 175
  growth from life to life 84-86, 87-88
  noise of, and hearing the soul 193
  subliminal 25
  yoga impossible by power of 109
Moksha 130
Mukti 111

N

Nature
  way of progress 90
Nirvāna 130

O

Overhead planes 38
Overmind, the
  and inspiration 189
  beings of, and psychic being 37, 50

P

Pāpa
  and *punya* 131, 139
Parā prakṛti 16
Parameshwara, the 14
Parents
  influences of, and psychic life 150
Personality
  and person 134, 134-36
  survival of 134, 135
Pitṛyāna 130
Planes
  psychic and spiritual 36
Power 190
Prakriti 7, 16, 79
  and Purusha 11
Pranamaya Purusha *see under* Purusha
Progress
  and decline 93
  and individualisation 95
  and manifestation 94
  from life to life 87, 89
  of the individual 71
  of the psychic 87, 89, 90, 91
  only upon earth 93
  way Nature progresses 90
Psychic *see* Psychic, the
Psychic
  and spiritual 36-37
  usage of the word 3, 4, 5, 6, 9, 32fn
Psychic, the (soul/psychic element/

psychic essence/psychic) 3, 4, 11-12, 53
  in the plant and animal 11
Psychic being ("the psychic")
  action/influence of 52-56, 97
  action in ordinary life 59
  aim of 95
  always balanced 184
  always pure 35
  and abnormal phenomena 3, 4, 7, 32fn
  and assimilation of experience 136, 138
  and beings of vital world 165fn
  and choice of conditions of rebirth 80, 84-85, 137-50
  and choice of sex in rebirth 143
  and concentration 117
  and conversion 107
  and delight-soul 188
  and difficulties 186
  and divine Work 86, 88, 92
  and ease and peace 183
  and emotion 191
  and evil life 36
  and evolution 75, 78
  and faith 44-45
  and fear of dying 179-80
  and formation of new body 86
  and happiness 184
  and heart centre 166
  and hostile forces 114
  and immortality 199
  and individualisation 95
  and inner Truth 173
  and inspiration 189
  and Intermediate Zone 109
  and Liberation 111
  and matter 37, 50
  and memory of past lives 134, 137, 151
  and non-evolutionary being 7
  and physical disabilities 35
  and birth-environment 129
  and seances 133
  and sense of continuity 178-79
  and sense of immortality 178
  and solar plexus 9
  and successive experiences 95
  and suffering 125, 187-88
  and the Atman 19
  and the central being 18
  and the centres 168
  and the good, true, beautiful 18, 32, 55
  and the heart 6
  and the inner being 10
  and the Jivatman 14, 15, 20
  and the mineral, plant and animal 82
  and the physical 172
  and the soul 7, 8, 9, 10, 12, 14-15, 16
  and transformation 19, 104
  and understanding divine Love 190
  and will to realise the Divine 181-82
  and work of unifying the being 67

asleep in most cases 106
aspiration of 20
assimilation of experience 87
awakening of, and conversion 107
bringing/coming forward (to the front) 4, 5, 108, 110, 111, 112, 114, 120, 121, 151
centre of organisation 90
characteristic of man 175
communications from 43
consciousness of 113
contact with 23, 105 and sadhana 104
discovery of, and new possibilities 188
draws things which help 61
emerges slowly 114
expression of 180
formation of 19, 84
function of 49
going back to inferior consciousness 134
growth of, essential conditions for 99
guides the being 60
has a form 168, 170
in animals 78, 79, 171, 172
in children 171, 175
in fourth dimension 166
in plants 170
in the atom 169-70, 178
individualised in human being 50, 170
influence/action of 52-56, 99

inmost being 17
intervention of, in average people 151
intimation of 53
its culmination 80
kernel of its nature 38
knows spontaneously 43
location of 162
makes no mistake 66
meaning of 3, 4, 6, 7, 8
natural attitude of 14
of essence of Ananda 187
only upon earth 50, 169fn
opening of 116
opens rest of the nature 109
organises existences 62
organises experiences 95
progress of 85, 87, 89-90
real Man 28
realisation of 121
reason of its existence 49
sorrow of 123
starting-point of 163
time of coming after rebirth 129, 130
two aspects of 16, 38
uniting consciously with 186
veiled by its instruments 79
way of, of doing yoga 122
will of 49
withdrawal of 115
word "psychic" 4, 5, 9, 33fn
see also Chaitya Purusha; Inmost being; *cf.* Soul
Psychic change

meaning of 109
Psychic consciousness at work in life 61
Psychic discipline 66
Psychic emotion 186
Psychic entity 52, 99, 111, 120 135
   and evolution 54-57
   double 24
   ever-pure 52
Psychic fire 59
Psychic individualisation 170
Psychic intervention
   in life 153
Psychic law
   and reason 180
Psychic light 84, 148
Psychic-mental 21
Psychic personality/individuality 4, 5, 9, 12, 30, 31, 38, 79
   development of 96
Psychic-physical 21
Psychic poise 179
Psychic presence 80
   flower, first manifestation of 170
   identifying with 68
   in vegetal life 170
Psychic transformation 56, 111, 120
Psychic-vital 21
Psychic world 129, 130-31
   substance of 165-66
Puṇya
   and *pāpa* 131, 139
Purification
   and sadhana 110
Purusha(s) 5, 6, 7, 27, 79
   and Prakriti 11
   annamaya puruṣa 18
   Chaitya Purusha (*caitya puruṣa*) 6, 19, 31, 168
   five 105
   Kshara 16
   Manomaya Purusha (*manomaya puruṣa*) 5, 18
   physical 12
   Pranamaya Purusha (*prāṇamaya puruṣa*) 5, 18
   Purusha Antaratman 5

R

Rakshasic being
   possession by 36
Ramakrishna 14
Realisation
   and transformation 108
Reason 180
Rebirth/Reincarnation
   time taken for 139, 140
   with full memory 134
   common blunder about 135
Resistance
   and suffering 123-24

S

Sadhana
   and bringing forward the psychic being 111

danger in 110
purification and consecration in 108
when the psychic being is in front 120
Samatā 114
Seances
and the psychic being 133
Self-consecration *see* Consecration
Self-realisation
three steps of 103-104
Self, the 14
way of, in meeting suffering 123
see also Atman, the
Sex
line of, followed by soul 131
Sheaths 129, 132
Sincerity
and unification of being 182-83
Socrates 30
Solar plexus 9, 9fn
Soul 5, 6, 7, 9
action/influence of 52-56
active and asleep 195
always pure 35
and Catholic religion 80
and cultivation of body 86
and evolution 53-54
and "myself" 197
and power of control 193
and self-realisation 103
and suffering 123, 132
and the Atman 13
and the Divine 49
and the ghost 11
and the life 26
and the psychic being 8-10, 12, 14-15
and Truth, Good and Beauty 81
and vital activity, difference between 195-98
and voice of conscience 33
call of 22
cessation from birth 13
choice of body 144-47
coming forward 30
condition of, in psychic world 130
contact with 23-24
discovery of 103
double 24
emergence of 111
entering a new body 129
eyes, mirror of 176
feeling, in others 194
finding 196-97
going back to animal condition 133
growth of 81
immortality of 134
influence/action of 52-56
inmost 22
line of sex 131
meanings 21
nature of 28
of desire 27; *see also* Desire-soul
of plant or animal 11
role of 51

spark of the Divine 15, 19
true 28
true central being 111
voice of 193
see also Psychic, the; *cf.* Psychic being
Soul-personality 54, 56, 111
Spirit 13, 14
Spiritual
and psychic 36-37
Spiritual experience
converting mental seeking into 117-20
Spiritual presence
basis of control and protection 164
Sráddha 129
Subconscious influences 150
Subconscious, the
difficulties from 150
Subliminal, the 25, 30
Suffering
and evil 139
and resistance 123-24
indication of weak point 186
Supramental consciousness 80
Supramental transformation 105
Supermind, the
and inspiration 189

T

Taittiriya Upanishad 12, 105
Teacher
help of 120

Transformation
and realisation 108
psychic 58, 120
spiritual 121
supramental 105
triple 104-05
Truth
and the psychic 173
Truth, Good and Beauty 18, 32-33, 55, 81, 103, 112
Typal world 8

U

Unification of being 67
and sincerity 183
Upanishads 27

V

Vegetal life
psychic presence in 170
Virgil 135
Vital being 26
true 24
Vital sheath *see* Sheaths
Vital, the
from life to life 87-89, 89-91
noise of, and hearing the soul 192-93

W

Will
of the psychic 49

to realise the Divine 181
Woman
   and man, distinction between 172

Y

Yoga
   and emotion 191
   two ways of doing 122
Yogadrishti
   and memory of past lives 151

**Compilations from the works of
Sri Aurobindo and the Mother
by the same Editor**

Living Within
The Yoga Approach to
Psychological Health and Growth

The Psychic Being
Soul — Its Nature, Mission and Evolution

The Hidden Forces of Life

Growing Within
The Psychology of Inner Development

Looking from Within
A Seeker's Guide to Attitudes for Mastery and
Inner Growth

Powers Within

Living Words
Soul-Kindlers for the New Millennium

Our Many Selves:
Practical Yogic Psychology

Emergence of the Psychic:
Governance of Life by the Soul

The Yoga of Sleep and Dreams
The Night-School of Sadhana